RIPE FOR THE PICKING

THE INSIDE STORY OF THE NORTHERN BANK ROBBERY

Chris Moore

Gill & Macmillan

Gill & Macmillan Ltd
Hume Avenue, Park West, Dublin 12
with associated companies throughout the world
www.gillmacmillan.ie
© Chris Moore 2006
ISBN-13: 978 07171 4001 5
ISBN-10: 0 7171 4001 6
Typography design by Make Communication
Print origination by O'K Graphic Design, Dublin
Printed and bound by Nørhaven Paperback A/S, Denmark

This book is typeset in 10/12.5 Minion.

The paper used in this book comes from the wood pulp of
managed forests. For every tree felled, at least one tree is
planted, thereby renewing natural resources.

A CIP catalogue record for this book is available from the
British Library.

5 4 3 2 1

CONTENTS

01 | TIME FOR PEACE

'We're going to have to take you away for a period of twenty-four hours. Your family will be held for that time in the house and you have a very simple choice. The choice is that you co-operate with us, and your family will be fine. If you don't, they're dead. The choice for your family is that if they work with us, you're fine. If they don't, you're dead. It's as simple as that.'—KIDNAPPER TO CHRIS WARD

—

Christmas 2004 is just six days away. Although traditionally the season of peace and goodwill, in Northern Ireland this particular Christmas had seen the hopes of the local population for a peaceful settlement to the political deadlock dashed just a few days earlier. Expectations had been high that changes in the electoral landscape would see Sinn Féin and the Democratic Unionist Party (DUP), the two major power brokers in Northern Ireland and hitherto sworn political enemies, reach agreement on a historic deal. The sense of frustration and disappointment that such a deal had not been brokered and that not a single gesture signifying IRA disarmament had been forthcoming was perhaps all the more intense because of the time of year. Yet true to form, the people of Northern Ireland were preparing in spite of everything to set aside yet another political failure and to celebrate the Christmas season with family and friends . . .

At his family home on the Poleglass housing estate on the outskirts of west Belfast, avid Celtic supporter and football fan Chris Ward is looking forward to watching a Spanish League game on television with his father Gerry. The 23-year-old Northern Bank employee could afford to relax watching the

Spanish game, especially after the previous day when he had made the trip to Glasgow as a 'participating' fan to watch his beloved Celtic beat Dundee United.

Ward's mother, his brother Gerard and his brother's girlfriend Ursula are also in the house. Gerard and Ursula are in an upstairs room.

Thirty miles away in County Down, another Northern Bank official, Kevin McMullan, is relaxing with his wife Karen after spending the day at their bungalow near Loughinisland.

The small village of Loughinisland had been the scene of loyalist carnage some ten years earlier. The village pub, Heights Bar, had been crowded with more than two dozen drinkers on the Saturday night of 18 June 1994. The crowd had been watching Ireland beat Italy in New York in their first game in the 1994 World Cup finals. Their backs to the door, they had not seen death come calling in the form of masked UVF killers who opened fire with automatic weapons on the unsuspecting football fans. Six Catholic men died as the gunmen peppered the bar with gunfire from an AK-47 and a Czech-made rifle. The killings were undoubtedly a revenge attack for the INLA's murder two days earlier of UVF member Colin Craig on Belfast's Shankill Road, an incident in which two other UVF men, David Hamilton and Trevor King, had also died. In typical terrorist doublespeak, the UVF tried to justify its sectarian slaughter in Loughinisland by alleging the bar was being used for a 'republican function'. Of course, it was arrant nonsense.

But the incident had devastated the mainly Catholic village. Previously unknown Loughinisland had become the latest small community to have its name thrown into the ever-increasing lexicon of Northern Irish place names which had become synonymous with sectarian murder. Names like Greysteel and Teebane and Enniskillen . . .

Ten years on, and Loughinisland is once again about to have its name in headlines—but this time for a very different reason.

Kevin McMullan and Chris Ward work together at the Northern Bank's headquarters in Belfast. As they get on with their various Sunday routines at their respective homes, others are planning to disrupt their lives. Things will never be the same again for either of these two men.

The mobile phone networks are red-hot that Sunday for a group of ruthless criminals. These men have plans to treat themselves for Christmas. They're going to help themselves to somebody else's money—in very large amounts.

The experienced gang take every precaution to avoid detection. Speaking in code, they use unregistered mobile phones to avoid the pitfalls of the technology that could potentially give their game away to police.

The leader of the gang is a highly respected republican. As a man who has served time in the Maze Prison, he is highly skilled in the deadly art of psychological manipulation. No amount of training could have prepared prison officers for the type of psychological warfare they would face on the wings of the H-Blocks from paramilitary prisoners.

The timing of this bank raid will spark great debate, but as the gang leader knows, there is now an urgent imperative to get the job done without delay. For, although in the aftermath of the robbery the raid would be seen as a spectacular operation to mark the breakdown of the peace talks, the gang leader knows that the true reasons for its timing are very different. The raid has been in the planning phase for almost two years but now circumstances have created an unforeseen urgency.

The gang leader spends Sunday making sure everything is in place. The call he has been waiting for from the 'insider' at the Northern Bank has put him on full alert.

The nucleus of the robbery gang is an experienced team . . . a team that has worked successfully together on similar operations. But this job requires a bigger team—as many as twenty-five to thirty. The men have been divided into small units to carry out specific tasks. Each unit knows only enough to complete its part of the operation. Only a tried and trusted few know all of the details. The time for rehearsals and dry runs is over—it is time for action.

The two men with the keys to the cash-laden vault at Northern Bank headquarters in Belfast have been identified by the 'insider' as Chris Ward from Poleglass and Kevin McMullan from

Loughinisland. For the plan to work, Ward and McMullan must be on duty as the key-holders to the bank's cash vault on the day of the robbery. The leader of the gang is known as a meticulous planner. Satisfied that everything is in place, he gives the order for the operation to go ahead as planned.

The leader has his teams of men take up position in the west Belfast area, in County Down and even in south Armagh. In the lead-up to the fateful day, members of the gang have divided their time between their families and the top-secret preparations for the Christmas bank heist to end all bank heists. They have checked their weapons, moved them to the correct locations and have studied over and over again the detail they now know about the bank, how it operates and the vital information about key members of the bank staff.

There is a knock at Chris Ward's front door. The television football game is still being played. It is close to 10 p.m. Normally Ward's father, Gerry, answers the door. But as Gerry is sitting comfortably on the sofa with his feet up, Chris decides to go to the door himself.

Standing on the doorstep is a man who tells Ward that he wants to see him 'about Celtic'. As assistant treasurer of the local Éire Go Brach Celtic Supporters Club, for Chris this is not an unusual occurrence. The man asks if he can chat to Chris Ward in the kitchen and is invited into the house. But Ward quickly notices a second man entering his home. Both visitors are unmasked but manage to keep their faces fairly well covered using hats and their coat collars.

By now, alarm bells are ringing for Chris Ward. Things turn ugly. The two strangers threaten him: soon his entire family is being held hostage.

The situation is no better thirty miles away in Loughinisland. It's an icy cold Sunday evening when Karen McMullan answers a knock at her front door. There, two men in police uniforms confront her. They have bad news: apparently a relative has been killed in a traffic accident.

With this lie, the men gain access to the McMullan home. Once inside, the phoney officers produce a gun and put it to

Kevin McMullan's head. They tie him up and throw him onto a mattress. Then they lay it on the line for the two terrified captives: 'Co-operate—or die.' Kevin watches as the gang force Karen to put on a boiler suit. He sees them bind her hands before placing a hood over her head.

He is absolutely petrified. His heart is thumping so hard he thinks it is going to burst out of his body as he watches the robbers remove his wife from the room. As they have been instructed, the kidnappers attempt to reassure the McMullans that if they co-operate, no one will come to any harm.

Now the robbers have control of two Northern Bank employees. And, crucially, it is the two members of staff who have the keys to one of the richest treasure vaults in the country: the Northern Bank headquarters' cash centre.

Back in Poleglass, Chris Ward knows there is something seriously wrong. His worst fears are confirmed when one of the intruders informs him:

> We know who you are. We know everything about you. We know who your family is. We know everything about them and we're here about your job.

> We're going to have to take you away for a period of twenty-four hours. Your family will be held for that time in the house and you'll have a very simple choice. The choice is that you co-operate with us, and your family will be fine. If you don't, they're dead. The choice for your family is that if they work with us, you're fine. If they don't, you're dead. It's as simple as that.

The two men manhandle the young bank official back into the family living room, where a third member of the gang is sitting with Chris's father. Despite his own panic, Ward tries to calm his family down. As he's telling his father not to worry, his mother hears the commotion and hurries downstairs. Despite her son's reassurances, what she sees in the living room soon has her in tears.

By now, Ward is, naturally, worried on two fronts—for his own personal safety, and for that of his family, who will undoubtedly suffer if anything goes wrong. Yet, up to this point, he has not actually seen a gun.

Before he is taken from the house, there is a remarkable incident. The intruders want the Ward family to underwrite their promise to co-operate by swearing on a holy picture. As he would later explain, in Chris Ward's view and that of his family, 'once you swear on a holy picture, then you are giving someone your word.'

In 1983, Brendan 'Bik' McFarlane, one of the Maze Prison escapees at the time, had used the same technique when he forced a Christian family living near the jail to swear on the Bible they would not raise the alarm for seventy-two hours.

Sectarian murderer McFarlane, a one-time student for the Catholic priesthood, was a member of the IRA gang that carried out a gun and bomb attack on the Bayardo Bar on Belfast's Shankill Road in August 1975. That attack had left five people dead—none of them involved in paramilitary activity. When, in September 1983, McFarlane escaped along with thirty-nine other republican prisoners, he found himself making his getaway with a group of eight other men in a stolen car. They decided they had to get rid of the stolen vehicle to avoid detection by hundreds of mobilised police and soldiers.

McFarlane's group, which included Seamus McElwaine, later to be shot dead by the British Army's SAS, took over the home of a Protestant couple, Ian and Doreen McFarlane (no relation), near Dromore in County Down. When it was time for McFarlane and the other IRA escapees to leave, they found themselves in a dilemma.

As McFarlane explained in 1993 during filming for a UTV documentary marking the tenth anniversary of the escape from the Maze:

> *We had established earlier on in the evening that the McFarlanes were a good Christian family—they had been talking about their church hall, and prayer meetings etc.—so I felt that to try to avoid any of the other options open to us, if we could get them to swear on their principles so that they wouldn't go to the police*

for seventy-two hours, we would be prepared to accept it.

Now I know a lot of people wouldn't go for it, but I didn't want to leave anybody behind, I didn't want to have to take anybody in the house with us, and, well, I didn't want to tie them up. So if they were prepared to swear on the Bible, then I was prepared to accept that, and I gave them the guarantee that if they did that, then nobody would be harmed.

So once the family had taken their oath on the Bible, promising not to alert the police for at least seventy-two hours, McFarlane and his group left the house:

We took a number of things. We took some food, I mean not a lot. We took two rucksacks. We also took some heavy clothing like sweaters, tracksuit bottoms and I think . . . yeah, the two young lads had a scout map, and a small compass, and a radio. No, we didn't steal them at all . . . I wrote a receipt of whatever we took, an inventory of everything that we took, and I signed it and I gave it to the woman of the house. I told her that in the event that she was prepared to go and contact the republican movement in Belfast, that because of the signature they would reimburse her, at least to the relative value of what we had taken.

McFarlane said that Seamus McElwaine and one of the other escapees were dealing with Mrs McFarlane, and he recalled:

Both of them were extremely polite with her: very, very courteous. I think that she saw in us a group of people who were not monsters like the media and the NIO or the British portrayed. When I left the house, I just apologised for the inconvenience, said that I understood that it was a very, very traumatic experience, and sincerely wished them well for the future.

So apparently the principle of getting a family to swear on something holy was nothing new to the IRA, but was a technique that had been tried and tested long before the Ward family were asked to give their word on a holy picture.

Meanwhile, at the Ward home the intruders get ready to take the young bank official away from his family. They tell him to fetch his bank uniform. Ward goes upstairs to find his uniform and packs it carefully into a bag. Once this is done, Ward, still unaware of his destination, is then escorted to a waiting car outside the family home. As he leaves the house, he hears his mother crying.

Outside, Ward is instructed to lie down on the back seat of what he notes is a three-door vehicle. It's at this moment that Chris Ward catches sight of a gun for the first time. The driver turns around and points the barrel of a handgun at the terrified young bank official, who turns his head away, panicked and totally terrified. The gunman tells him to expect to be in the car for about forty-five minutes and that he should think only of his family. He's to remain calm and it's suggested he even try to imagine that he isn't in the car at all.

Naturally, Ward complies with the demands of the armed driver. He knows he is being taken at gunpoint because he's a supervisor at the bank, someone who on occasion holds the keys to the vaults at the bank's headquarters' cash distribution and sorting centre. It's obvious his kidnappers have devised some kind of plan to rob the bank.

But Ward also realises that he's unfortunate to have been caught up in their plans like this. He's not the official originally chosen for tomorrow's early shift. On Friday afternoon, the rota had been published and circulated. Ward was not rostered for duty on Monday. The change of rota was made late on Friday at Ward's request. But how did these men know about that?

The main concern for the young Poleglass man is the welfare of his family. It is dark and he is frightened. He fears that these men are going to kill them because for whatever security reason, the robbery of the bank's headquarters just isn't going to be possible.

Ward is frantically trying to work out in his head how the kidnappers can make this robbery work. He can see no way of getting cash out of the vaults in the bank—at least not a way that would not raise the alarm. There are internal security doors, not to mention a security presence at all entrances. And there is absolutely no way the robbers could get a vehicle into the bullion bay because that is under observation at all times by security staff in their bullet-proof control room.

Suddenly, Ward's thoughts are interrupted by the driver's voice as the car draws to a halt. 'There's another car here, just get straight into it,' he's told. He moves the two steps necessary to get from one vehicle into the other—still unaware of his destination.

Now he is sitting in the passenger seat in the second car, not lying down as he had been in the first. He is told to look straight ahead at all times and under no circumstances to turn around or touch anything. He stares ahead into the darkness.

What happens next, just a few minutes into this second journey, startles him. The driver suddenly says something. 'Man in the back,' he says, according to Ward, 'You know what you're doing? You know what you have to do when you get to the house? You know there are sensors.'

The real shock for Ward comes when someone replies from the darkness of the seat behind him with just one word: 'Yep.' Ward did not notice anyone else in the vehicle and he is spooked, to say the least, by the presence of yet another unidentified kidnapper in the darkness behind him.

But by now he has worked out in his mind what is going on. Catching sight of a signpost for Loughinisland, he reckons this can only mean one thing: they're on their way to the home of his work colleague, Kevin McMullan.

Although they work together, Ward knows very little about McMullan. He remembers Kevin and Karen getting married recently. They opted to live out in the country near their families and miles away from the city and Poleglass. Ward himself is single, having recently split up with his girlfriend. His free time is mainly taken up with his activities as a supporter of Glasgow's Celtic. He thinks of his girlfriend and is glad in a way that they fell out recently: it will keep her out of all this turmoil.

In Loughinisland, Kevin McMullan is trying to come to terms with the events of the last few hours. Bound and helpless, Kevin can only watch as Karen is removed from the house. He hears the familiar noise of her car engine turn over. His hearing accentuated by fear, he listens intently as the car leaves the house, and he tries to work out what direction it is taking.

Of course, even though he can tell which way they turned as they left the driveway, he has no idea where Karen is being taken. He tries to fight back terrible thoughts, without success. The most frightening of all is the thought that he may never see her alive again. God knows what ordeal she will face. Thoughts for his own safety just do not occur to him. It is his wife's safety that preoccupies him. He feels so powerless.

Then Chris Ward is brought in. He doesn't have long to dwell on his thoughts because he's soon having his hands tied behind his back. Then he's shoved into a corner where he's instructed to stand still.

Ward remains like this for what he reckons is over an hour— maybe even an hour and a half. He is crying and thinking of his family. Eventually one of the kidnappers enters the room and tells Ward to follow him. He's led into a small room where Kevin is being held.

Ward is shocked to see his work colleague tied up and sitting on a mattress. Ward is told to sit down beside Kevin on the mattress. One of the gang kicks him and tells McMullan to get his workmate to calm down or someone will get hurt.

Ward manages to tell Kevin that 'they' have taken his family— his mother, father, brother—but before he can finish, Kevin tells him that his wife Karen has been taken away by 'them'. This is hard to take in, according to Ward. The scene is playing out in front of two masked men. In spite of coming from Poleglass in west Belfast, Ward has never seen masked men before. They scare him. And they want answers to questions about the bank and the security system.

Most of their questions are, apparently, directed at Kevin McMullan, the more senior of the two bank staff. Ward looks on in terror as the kidnappers exert intense psychological pressure with their relentless questioning.

The gang leader has carefully instructed his men to be firm with

the hostages, to make sure that they know that there will be serious
consequences if they refuse to co-operate. The success of the whole
operation depends on their ability to strike fear into their quarry.

It was a tried and tested method of psychological warfare which
had been used so effectively to facilitate the Maze Prison escape in
1983. Following the deaths of ten republicans on hunger strike in
1981, the prisoners had to create the impression inside the jail that
they had become 'model prisoners'.

Bewildered and confused, prison staff looked at people like Gerry
Kelly, 'Bik' McFarlane, Bobby Storey, Brendan Mead, Sean
McGlinchey and Tony McAllister all acting as orderlies and
wondered what was really going on. They had their suspicions, but
during the many months that the prisoners' 'conditioning' of the
prison staff continued, they were lured into relaxing and opting for
the easy life. But it was all a clever ruse by the prisoners in the
carefully planned escape bid. On the day of the escape, there were
too many prisoners in the 'circle'—more than the regulations
allowed. This had only become possible because of the carefully
orchestrated mind games being played by the republican prisoners.

In jail, enormous pressure could be applied to an individual
officer by a simple casual remark, along the lines of: 'I believe your
missus still shops at Crazy Prices in Dunmurry every Friday night
in that old battered Escort . . . what's the number . . . COI something
. . . your daughter is beautiful, isn't she?'

Such casual remarks would suffice to make the 'screw' aware that
his personal details were known to the paramilitary prisoners he
was looking after every day. And that in itself was often enough to
give the prisoners the kind of edge that allowed them to rule their
own roost . . . well, that and the fact that the Provos had murdered
a number of prison staff when it suited their 'political' needs.

Now similarly ruthless methods are being used on the families
of two bank employees.

Karen McMullan is certainly experiencing fear as she is driven
around in the dark, blindfolded and therefore totally unaware of
her destination. Sensory deprivation is terrifying. Karen's mind
struggles to find order among the rush of chaotic thoughts:
'Where are they taking me? What will they do to Kevin? Are they

going to rape me? Beat me? Or worse? All these thoughts course through her mind over and over again—even though the men in the car emphasise that she will be all right if she doesn't attempt to scream or raise the alarm in any way. She is told that to do so would also be detrimental to the health of her husband. Karen McMullan is now facing the kind of psychological warfare faced by prison staff in the H-Blocks.

Back at the McMullan home too, the kidnappers are continuing to subject their captives to intense psychological pressure. They set about pressing Ward and McMullan for information about the Northern Bank cash centre: the staff arrangements, the layout of the centre and, most crucially of all, how the security systems operate.

How many security doors between the cash centre and the street outside? How many security staff on duty at night? When do they finish their shift? Where are the CCTV cameras positioned? Will it seem unusual if McMullan and Ward remain behind after the others have gone? What are the security access codes?

Sometimes the kidnappers seem satisfied with an answer, but five minutes later they ask the same question in a different way, as if trying to trip up the hostages. At times they challenge a previous reply, or pit one victim's answer against the other's: 'Well, Kevin, that's not what your friend Chris here told us on the way here. He said that there was no camera at that location. Now, let's have a straight answer here. Stop messing us about.'

Ward and McMullan are now feeling the pressure of question after question about the bank. At one stage, the gang get very nasty, shouting as they accuse Kevin of looking over at the panic button installed in his home by the bank as a security measure to help combat situations just like this one. Kevin assures them he has no such thoughts in his head. He doesn't want anything to happen to his wife. The kidnappers settle down again and resume the relentless questioning.

What amazes the two hostages most is the extent of the knowledge the kidnappers have of their victims and their families. They also have considerable knowledge of the bank. The robbers have obviously spent time doing their homework. To Ward, the whole idea that he and his family may very well have been under observation for some time is really disturbing. The kidnappers know everyone's name—even that of his brother's girlfriend. They *have* to have been watching to know as much as they do.

It occurs to McMullan and Ward that these men had sufficient knowledge of the bank to know when to target them: they evidently knew when they would be on duty together—and in possession of the keys to the vault. In trying to figure out how they could possibly have known this, McMullan remembers something that makes it all the more puzzling.

Thinking back to the previous Friday, just two days earlier, he recalls that the rota putting him and Ward together had been altered at the last moment because Chris Ward had wanted to change his shift so that he would be on duty the next day, Monday. How could the gang of robbers have possibly known about this last minute change? Then the penny drops. Someone on the inside knew about the change and must have told the kidnappers. It was the only explanation. A colleague had set them up.

Once the questioning is finally over, the masked men separate the two exhausted and terrified bank officials. Ward is taken back to the kitchen and McMullan is returned to the small room with the mattress. One of the kidnappers tells them to get some sleep as they have a busy day ahead of them.

Chris Ward is struggling to think about how this daring raid can possibly be carried off. In the back of his mind is the thought that it is impossible. Someone will notice something and raise the alarm, and that would be beyond his control. He thinks of his family. He's convinced these men will carry out their threat to kill them if anything goes wrong. The kidnappers have left him in no doubt. The inner turmoil is crippling, the uncertainty devastating. Like Kevin McMullan, Ward gets little sleep that night.

With Ward and McMullan left to sleep, one of the kidnappers contacts the gang leader to inform him that their detailed quizzing of the two bank staff has not thrown up any unexpected anomalies.

The gang already had a detailed knowledge of the internal workings of the bank and they knew what to expect from Ward and McMullan. As it happens, the terrified bank staff have confirmed everything the gang knew about the bank, its security and their work routine. And most importantly of all, they are terrified enough to follow orders and go through with the robbery.

The leader reminds his men to keep the two hostages apart for as long as possible so they can't discuss and debate the issues. Before the two set off for work the next day, the kidnappers are to let them know they will be watched carefully. They must be in no doubt about the consequences of trying to get help.

The gang leader reminds his men that when they leave the McMullan home they must take every precaution to ensure they leave behind no tell-tale forensic clues. They are to wash and scrub up meticulously to remove any potentially damaging clues. Floors must be washed and all surfaces wiped with disinfectant or strong detergent. Their masks are to be worn at all times in front of the captives. That's as important as making sure Ward and McMullan experience the fear of God.

The two bank staff will be given mobile phones so that the kidnappers can remain in touch with them throughout the day. They have to understand and believe their families will die if they follow the bank's special security measures in the event of a kidnapping—like making use of the special telephone hotline provided by the bank for staff vulnerable to kidnap and the security arrangements subsequently activated which have been devised not to arouse suspicion among the kidnappers that the police have become aware of what is going on. This system has been used in the past to ensure that kidnap victims survive the ordeal and that the kidnappers get some kind of payout to keep them happy. Ward and McMullan, however, will set off for work the next morning without the slightest intention of availing of the bank's security procedures. They want above all to see their loved ones again.

02 | STEALING TO SURVIVE

Karen McMullan is distressed and disoriented. The instinct for survival keeps her moving. She's in tears as she stumbles towards freedom. She has no idea what has happened to her husband and when or if she will see him again. Then she sees lights in the distance. Now her mind begins to focus on getting to the house ahead of her, on the edge of Drumkeeragh Forest.

It is 6 a.m. on Monday 20 December 2004. The kidnappers are preparing to leave the McMullan home. Before they go, they remind Ward and McMullan once again that they are risking the lives of their families if they deviate from the plan outlined to them the night before.

Once the gang leave, the two bank employees are alone and have a chance to talk about the traumatic events of the previous eight hours. Both of them have been dreading the arrival of daylight and the journey to Belfast, where they will be expected to playact their way through the day, keeping up a façade of normality in front of their work colleagues.

To act normally whilst inwardly experiencing fear and turmoil about what would happen to loved ones should anything go wrong is a terrifying prospect. For Kevin McMullan there is only the awful memory of when he last saw his wife Karen and the thought that even now, he has no idea of where she has been taken or what she may have undergone in the meantime.

Chris Ward knows where his family is being held, but he too is filled with anxiety at the thought of what will happen to them if the gang's plan doesn't succeed. What if one of his co-workers sees a bead of sweat or senses his nervousness and raises the alarm?

Finally it is time to go to work: both men are due to begin their shifts at midday. Kevin McMullan drives. The two men are afraid to look behind. They are afraid they may be under observation by other members of the gang of kidnappers. They must have been 'watched' before: this was the only conclusion they could draw from the fact that the gang of robbers knew precisely when and where to strike against them and their families. Now their minds are racing with thoughts of who may be watching them now, at this very moment, to make sure they do everything they have been told to do. They dare not think of doing anything that could be seen as an attempt to raise the alarm. They drive along towards work, among other commuters making their way from rural County Down into Belfast, knowing that the day will be a daunting ordeal, to say the least. By the time they reach the city centre, the adrenaline has both men in a state of high alert. A day of nervous tension looms.

McMullan drops Chris Ward off along the Dublin Road as instructed by the kidnappers. They are to get into work as normal —and that does not entail the two men arriving together, of course. They enter the bank buildings separately and set about their usual daily routine. Understandably, it is not easy for either of them—but both men are driven by the desire to ensure the safety of their families.

Throughout the day, Ward's family remain in their own home, guarded by members of the gang, while Kevin McMullan's wife Karen, dressed in a boiler suit and with a hood covering her eyes, is being held in a building somewhere far removed from the family home. No matter how many times her kidnappers assure her that she will be safe if things go according to plan, nothing can assuage the sheer terror she is feeling.

Chris and Kevin get on with work. No one around them seems to sense that there is anything wrong. Both men are aware that the Northern Bank has special procedures for events just like this. Staff are expected to call a designated number if they find themselves in a situation where they or their families are under duress. But for Ward and McMullan, the kidnappers have the upper hand and pose such a very real threat to their loved ones that neither even contemplates making such a move. Without intending any disrespect to his employers, Ward admitted after the event that in his view, the bank's idea that if you are kidnapped you must never ever pay out but instead telephone the number specially set up for such eventualities was 'Superman stuff'. You would only do such a thing if you sincerely believed that 'Superman' was going to fly through the window to beat the gang off and save the kidnapped families. As Ward sees it, the reality is very different. Money and the financial interests of his employers are secondary to the health and welfare of his family. The truth is that there is no real choice involved.

Throughout the day the two bank employees are constantly contacted by the robbers on the mobile phones supplied for that purpose. During the long night at the McMullan family home, they were instructed by the robbers to carry out a plan intended to reassure the gang that everything is still on course. The two bank officials must deliver a bagful of cash—£1m in fifties and hundreds—to one of the gang members. And they must do so shortly after everyone else has left the building. Ward and McMullan have been told to stuff the cash into Chris Ward's sports bag. McMullan has been instructed by the kidnappers to send home a porter and the three other members of staff before 6 p.m.

So, once all the other staff have left the building, earlier than usual, Ward and McMullan begin to follow their instructions to the letter, placing as many £50 and £100 notes into the sports bag as they can manage. Initially, the gang wanted Kevin, the more senior of the two as sector manager, to deliver the bag. But according to Ward's subsequent account, Kevin pointed out that his leaving and re-entering the bank would raise questions and might attract attention. So it was agreed that Chris Ward would deliver the 'sweetener'.

The two bank staff finally manage to cram just over £1m inside the sports bag, which Ward then slings over his shoulder. He comes up from the basement where the cash office is located, gets buzzed through the two sets of internal security doors and simply walks out of the bank through the main staff door, turning left down Wellington Street. No one stops him or searches the bag he casually carries out of the very focal point of all the bank's security systems—the vaults where the bank's millions are stored. Chris Ward later describes this escape with over a million pounds as 'real freaky'.

Once safely out of the bank, Ward has been told to use the mobile phone provided by the robbers to contact another member of the gang to report that he has managed to get away unimpeded. He makes the call and receives further instructions: to walk to the end of Wellington Street to a bus stop in Upper Queen Street and wait there. He sits down, placing the bag beside him. Out of the corner of his eye, he notices someone move towards him. He glances up but, like the men at his house, the man who approaches him is wearing a hat and has covered up so that his face cannot be seen. Ward looks away, keeping his head down as the man gets closer. The man then makes some remark about Christmas, feigning normal conversation. Then he asks Ward if he has something to give him for Christmas. The bag with the cash is handed over and the man disappears in the direction of Castle Street. The robber has escaped with £1m in cash. Ward returns to the bank empty-handed.

He re-enters the bank through the staff door. And oddly enough, security staff do not notice that he is returning without the sports bag he had over his shoulder when leaving a short time before. Soon he's back with Kevin, who has been sitting alone in the bank's cash centre awaiting his return. The two already know their next move. It is time to prepare to move cash out of the safe.

News of the safe delivery of the £1m 'sweetener' is passed on to the gang leader. He has already made the decision, based on the afternoon conversations between the gang and the two bank staff, that the raid is to go ahead. There appear not to be any hindrances to the plan, and the tea-time delivery of the cash in the sports bag is the final confirmation that the two bank staff are following orders. Even before Ward delivered the cash in Belfast city centre, the boss has been in touch with his men in south Armagh, telling them it is safe enough to set off for Belfast in the white van that will be used to collect cash, in the guise of rubbish, from the bank.

The men in the van have been told not to enter the bank under any circumstances and that they are to remain in disguise—wigs and baseball caps—at all times, so as not to be picked up on the monitors inside the bank. They are instructed that if any problem should arise, they should drive the van to a designated place in the city and lay up until the difficulties are cleared.

As it happens, there is no cause for any diversion from the original plan. It is all systems go by the time they reach the outskirts of Belfast.

Back in the bank, Ward and McMullan are staring at a number of green crates of brand new Northern Bank notes. They have been instructed to bring out twenty-four of these crates—which contain new £20 and £50 notes—into the bullion bay area, which is where the money is routinely delivered and collected by established security companies such as Securicor.

Generally, Securicor vans would reverse into the bullion bay —an area under the control and watchful eyes of security staff in the control room. The bullion bay is located off Wellington Street: double doors open onto the street and once a delivery van is safely parked inside the bay, these doors close. Thus the van is sealed in a sterile area in the direct line of vision of security staff in the control room. The inner doors are generally opened only to facilitate the loading and unloading of cash brought up from the cash office in the basement in the company of a security guard and two bank officials.

A few yards down the street there is another set of double doors—the entrance to the underground car park for staff. Here two security staff patrol the street outside to check vehicles coming in and out and to make sure it is kept clear for easy access by the security vans. The two guards on duty outside the bank building—one stationed outside the double doors to the bullion bay and the other at the Queen Street end of Wellington Street— keep in contact using walkie-talkies.

But the robbers intend to do things differently. They make it clear to Ward and McMullan that they will not be bringing their vehicle inside the bank building, but that they will remain in the street outside. The bank officials are told to inform security that a company will be calling that evening to collect rubbish from the cash centre. Security should also be forewarned that Ward and McMullan themselves will be bringing the rubbish up to the bullion bay on trolleys.

Down in the basement of the bank, Ward and McMullan follow orders. They begin loading trolleys with the green boxes of new bank notes. With no camera watching them and with all the other staff already at home or Christmas shopping, their actions go unobserved. They make four runs in total through the labyrinth of corridors and security doors to the bullion bay. To disguise what they are really doing, they place some broken office furniture, old cardboard boxes and broken note counters on top of the trolleys. They also stuff used notes into black bin-liners and place them on top of the boxes of notes—even placing some wastepaper on top of the used notes inside the plastic bags, just in case security staff should happen to peek inside.

Having been told what to expect, security staff buzz open the two sets of internal doors leading out of the cash centre to the bullion bay as Ward and McMullan push and pull the trolleys through. On four separate runs, the two bank officials leave the trolley at the bullion bay double doors leading to the street— right under the eyes of the security staff in the control centre.

So, now that the money is safely out of the vault area and is sitting waiting for collection by the robbers behind the locked double doors of the bullion bay, Ward makes his next move as instructed. For the second time that evening, he steps out of the bank onto the street outside, leaving as he had done earlier in the day through the staff entrance. In order to get there, he leaves McMullan standing by the trolleys. Once he is on the street, and out of earshot, he uses the mobile phone supplied by the robbers to make contact with one of the gang.

The gang leader has good reason to be pleased. The County Down unit have Karen McMullan safely under 'wraps' at a secret location not that far from her home. She, of course, has been disoriented on the journey, deprived of her sight by the use of a couple of pieces of Sellotape over her eyes. The intention was that she could not see and, more importantly, that anyone looking in through the windows of the car being used to transport her would not notice the tape. Less obvious than a blindfold or hood, this was a proven technique used many times on journalists curious enough to seek out a meeting with the IRA at the height of the conflict.

Throughout the day, members of the gang have maintained contact with and kept up the pressure on the two bank officials. The leader is now satisfied that everything is in order for the final big push at the bank building. The van, with an automated tailgate to lift the heavy load of cash, will be arriving at the bank in a short time.

Ward tells the gang member at the other end of the phone that the money is ready for collection. Once he has finished his call, Ward walks to the Centra supermarket nearby and buys a couple of bottles of Coca-Cola to make security staff think he has just been on a break.

Ward returns to the bank building—through the staff entrance again, back through the cash centre in the basement, up in the lift and through the interlocked security doors where he finds McMullan waiting. He hands McMullan a bottle of Coke: things have to look normal to the security staff watching on CCTV. They stand talking for the benefit of the cameras.

When the van arrives, security staff alert Ward and McMullan. One of the security men even pauses for a chat with the two bank officials, who are by now feeling the strain of the day's events. They are all too aware that all it will take is for one of the security staff to open one of the cases on the trolleys—and they will be history. Even worse, their families will be history.

But they brazen it out. Both men are only grateful that security is lax enough to allow the robbers' plan to succeed. It takes only fifteen minutes to load the van with the cash-laden trolleys. Two of the gang actually get out of the vehicle wearing the delivery service uniforms and fleeces, as well as wearing wigs and caps.

Before driving off with the first load, one member of the gang hands Ward two rolls of black-coloured cling-film to wrap around trolleys in order to disguise them. He tells the young

Poleglass man, 'You've fifteen minutes to fill as many cages as you can with twenty pound notes'. According to Ward, it is only now that the bank officials realise that the gang intends coming back for a second load.

As the van disappears down the street, Ward and McMullan go about the business of preparing more trolleys for the robbers. But with only fifteen minutes to spare, they only manage to fill two of the trolleys, which are similar to the kind of trolleys used by supermarket staff when re-stocking shelves. With a growing sense of urgency, they use the rolls of black cling-film to wrap around the cages of the trolleys to keep security staff from discovering what is really inside.

Ward and McMullan have concerns about taking the two cages in the lift to the bullion bay floor level. From the lift they would have to push the cages through the interlocking security doors and the sterile area where security staff have a full view of everything.

But getting to the bullion bay before the gang arrive to collect the second load will be risky. Ward and McMullan fear that leaving the two cages of cash under the gaze of the security staff in the control room overlooking the bullion bay is a risk not worth taking. They desperately devise a plan to overcome this difficulty: they will phone the control room and tell security staff to expect the white van to return soon and that when it arrives, they should let them know, and they (Ward and McMullan) will bring the 'rubbish' straight up immediately. Even having taken this extra precaution, Ward and McMullan really fear that getting the second load on the two caged trolleys out through security is going to be impossible.

When the white van pulls up outside the bank a second time, security staff ring down to the cash office and alert the two bank officials that it has returned for the second load of rubbish. Nervous, Ward and McMullan set off towards the lift, the interlocking security doors and the bullion bay—convinced that this time their ruse will be rumbled. But they needn't have worried. This time security guards look on as around £10m is shoved out under their noses and into the street for loading on to the gangsters' white van.

The reality about security that night at the Northern Bank is that it was so relaxed that had the gang of robbers returned for a third load they might well have got away with that as well. In fact, they could have emptied the entire vault. As it was, they escaped with £26m.

Having despatched the robbers with almost £30m, Ward and McMullan return to the vault and lock up as normal. They set the alarms as usual—doubtless a surreal experience, given that this was a prime example of locking the stable door after the horse has bolted. But the act of locking up and setting off for home is also a relief. They have obeyed the gang of robbers and can now return to their families.

They have been instructed to drive first to Ward's home in Poleglass, and so they set off. It's a short journey—only a few miles from Belfast city centre through the late-night Christmas shopping traffic to west Belfast and on to Poleglass. But it's a worrying trip for both men. They still have very real concerns about whether or not the gang will hold up their end of the deal and leave their families unharmed. They have no idea of what awaits them in the Ward family home. Would the gang still be in the Ward home? Or would they have received word from the other gang members that the robbery had been a success and it was time to return to base? Would Karen McMullan be there? Why else would they be sending Kevin to Chris's house?

McMullan parks his car outside the Ward family home. The two men get out and head for the front door. Ward knocks. His mother shouts out: 'Who is it?' 'It's me, Mummy,' Ward replies. As the door opens, Ward can see his whole family sitting inside and for him at least there is some relief. But that still leaves Kevin McMullan in a distressed state of mind. There's no sign of Karen.

Masked men are still in the Ward house and they usher everyone into the kitchen, instructing them to remain there until notified otherwise. The reunited Ward family huddle together in the kitchen along with McMullan. Outside in the living room, the masked men are making sure they clean up every forensic trace. Once the masked men leave the premises a few minutes later, the

Wards comfort Kevin McMullan.

McMullan leaves the house about twenty minutes after the gang. As he's unfamiliar with the area, a member of the Ward family drives ahead of McMullan to ensure he safely negotiates his way to the more familiar route out of Belfast to Loughinisland. He then has a long, lonely journey to his home in Loughinisland to discover what has happened to Karen.

Karen McMullan's ordeal is nearly over. As the men in Poleglass are cleaning up any traces of their presence—scrubbing all the worktops in the kitchen, removing glasses and cups they used— Karen's kidnappers instruct her to get ready to leave. At around 9 p.m. Karen's eyes are covered again and she is taken to her car. One of her captors takes the wheel.

Eventually they stop the car and tell Karen it is time for her to get out. They set her free in a wooded area. They then drive off—but only a short distance. Parked in a remote spot, they set about destroying all forensic traces by setting fire to Karen's car. A second car arrives to collect them and the gang leave the scene.

Karen McMullan is distressed and disoriented. The instinct for survival keeps her moving. She's in tears as she stumbles towards freedom. She has no idea what has happened to her husband and when or if she will see him again. Then she sees lights in the distance. Now her mind begins to focus on getting to the house ahead of her, on the edge of Drumkeeragh Forest. It's almost 10 p.m. —twenty-four hours since the kidnappers arrived at her front door. She is now knocking on the front door of strangers herself seeking help. The family are shocked to see a young woman in such a distressed state. They bring her into the warmth of their home.

At five past ten, the family contact police to say a woman has just arrived at their house dressed in a boiler suit, obviously very distressed and disorientated, saying that she had been kidnapped, her husband works in a bank and that he is still missing. The police respond at once. When they arrive at the house and see Karen McMullan's obvious distress, they send for an ambulance which takes the released hostage to Downpatrick hospital for treatment.

The police send officers to the woman's house in Loughinisland. When they arrive, they are met by Kevin McMullan, who has just

arrived home from Belfast. McMullan quickly briefs the police on
the events of the past twenty-four hours. The full significance of the
robbery has not yet become obvious to the police, as the families in
Loughinisland and Belfast are so traumatised that it is difficult to
form an accurate picture of exactly what has happened.

At around 11 p.m., as Kevin McMullan arrives at his home,
Ward, back in Poleglass, is following the gang's orders and ringing
999. He tells police: 'Look, there's been a very, very serious
robbery and I had a horrendous ordeal.' When asked who he
thought had robbed the bank, Ward tells them he has no idea.

When police officers at the McMullan home in Loughinisland
and at the Ward home in Belfast make contact with each other,
the full significance of the biggest bank robbery ever in the British
Isles becomes clear.

The Chief Executive of the Northern Bank, Don Price, is
contacted at home. His first concern is for the welfare of his staff.
At this stage he has no idea just how bad this is going to be. He
raises the alarm with other staff. While he's doing that, police
phonelines are red-hot, as senior detectives are contacted at home
and told to report immediately for duty. Soon the Chief
Constable of the Police Service of Northern Ireland (PSNI), Hugh
Orde, is being briefed by his senior officers and he's stunned by
the scale of the robbery. He quickly orders the formation of a
large team of over forty detectives.

In charge of the team is Det. Supt Andy Sproule, an officer
with twenty-eight years' service who will be retiring in six
months' time. His first task is to secure the scenes of crime.
Initially there are four of these: the bank, the forest near the
McMullan family home where Mrs McMullan's car has been
burned out, and the two houses where the kidnappers held their
hostages prior to the robbery.

From the very outset it is clear to the investigating officers that
this is an inside job. From what little they have been able to
establish at this early stage, it is clear the robbers knew the routine
of the bank and its staff, even to the extent of knowing which staff
to target on this particular weekend. The whole operation bears
the hallmarks of a particular gang that have orchestrated a series

of other robberies involving the kidnapping of people at gunpoint while family members are forced to help in the robberies.

In circumstances like these, the investigating detectives must start with the source of the information about the robbery—and so Ward and McMullan must be regarded as potentially being involved until they are cleared. As one former senior detective confirms, what is done in the first twenty-four hours of an investigation is crucial. 'It is like a heart attack—what resources you choose to send to it, and where these are deployed, are vital to a positive outcome of an investigation.'

But from the outset, the police investigation is hampered. The robbers have taken great care to remove all forensic traces—and without forensic evidence, proving who was or was not involved is extremely difficult and can ultimately hasten a live enquiry towards the cold case file.

As soon as news of the robbery appeared in the media, the political game of laying blame began. As would be expected, unionists pointed the finger at the indignant republican movement. The police and the bank began searching for clues in a different sort of blame game. They wanted to establish who was involved, what help they may have had from the inside and also, of course, the reasons why the bank's security measures failed to pick up on the robbery. And while the robbers themselves appeared not to have given any obvious clues as to what organisation, if any, they belonged to, the police seemed to determine very quickly that the raid was the work of a criminal gang with IRA connections that had been active in this kind of crime for some years.

Chris Ward recalled members of the gang mentioning 'previous robberies'. As he would later tell the BBC *Spotlight* programme:

> They mentioned to Kevin previous robberies. The Strabane robbery, the Ulster Bank robbery, I think it was, but that was it. There was no organisation mentioned whatsoever. They referred back to Kevin by saying 'you know what happened

when the Ulster Bank guy, what happened when he paid out.
You know what happened to the Strabane . . .', there was an
Ulster Bank in Strabane incident or something like that. They
talked about it. 'You know what happened there . . .'

Whilst stopping short of saying they had involvement in
Strabane, they had let it be known that the method used there
had been successful and they wanted Ward and McMullan to
know what was expected of them if they wanted to see their
families alive again.

03 | GANG ON THE RUN

'In my opinion the Provisional IRA were responsible for this crime and all main lines of inquiry currently being undertaken are in that direction.'—PSNI CHIEF CONSTABLE HUGH ORDE, JANUARY 2005

—

It didn't take the police long to recognise the handiwork of the gang involved in the Northern Bank robbery—not because of any clues left behind but rather because of the lack of them. Local detectives had seen it all before from a gang that had given them the slip two or three times previously.

Experienced officers drafted on to the PSNI investigation team knew who was responsible but, as was so often the case during thirty bloody years of conflict, intelligence was insufficient for prosecution. No matter how much they might know about individual criminals, without physical and forensic evidence they simply could not pin enough on the perpetrators to make a successful prosecution.

As one senior detective told me: 'This mob are known to the police to be actively involved in major crimes but are so forensically aware that they make it more or less impossible for us to unearth the vital clues essential to prosecution and conviction.'

More troubling for the investigators and the Northern Bank on this occasion was the knowledge that the raid could not have taken place without inside help. Someone in the Northern Bank was a member of the gang of robbers.

Shortly after news of the robbery broke, I spoke to Jonty Brown, a detective who had served in the RUC and PSNI for thirty years, twenty-eight of them as a detective in CID. Brown knows an inside job when he sees one:

> There's no doubt, no doubt at all from the very instance it was
> made public knowledge that there was inside involvement.
> And this is what the police will pursue.

Brown solved many 'inside jobs' when he set up the Robbery
Squad for the greater Belfast area in 1994. He recalled:

> One case we solved was the robbery of Securicor cash in
> transit. Securicor were losing a lot of money in a number of
> robberies throughout the Province, but in the Belfast district
> we had one robbery in particular in which a million pounds
> was stolen by a Securicor guard working on the inside with
> what we believed was the UDA, and we were successful in our
> investigation of that. We managed to get a conviction for Keith
> Kenneth Winward, and the sentence he was handed out
> reflects the view the courts take of employees collaborating in
> such crimes. I believe Winward got fifteen years, and this was
> to send a signal to people who are working in positions of trust
> that breaches of that trust to facilitate criminals—armed
> criminals—are viewed very, very seriously by the courts.

Shortly after news of the robbery broke, I asked Brown if he could
help me understand where the bank raid investigators would
start. He explained:

> You've got to start at the very beginning, with the person who
> reports the crime . . . start there and work out. Each of those
> people are criminal suspects until they can be eliminated.
>   The ability of the police to bring to justice persons
> responsible, whether they are inside the bank or whether they
> are external to the bank, diminishes as time goes on. At the
> minute it's a very live enquiry, a very active enquiry, and those
> investigating have got a wealth of evidence to collect and
> procedures to go through as they try to identify and try to
> follow up the leads that are currently live.

There's no doubt the eyes of the world were now focused on the PSNI because the story of the robbery had international appeal, and was being described variously as the 'crime of the century' or 'the world's biggest ever haul of cash in a bank raid'.

The Northern Bank robbery was and is a major challenge to the investigating officers, putting them under immense pressure to solve the crime at a time when the entire force is reeling from criticisms. Not since the Omagh bomb investigation has the force been under such high-profile pressure to successfully prosecute the guilty.

The key questions for police were quickly identified. Who were the perpetrators? Who was involved on the inside? Why did we not get a hint from any of our informants? How did the bank security fail? What do we know about those responsible: how effective are they, for instance, in their criminal activities? What about their ability to disguise and remove forensics?

Det. Supt Andy Sproule told me what his first priorities were:

> Well, we start with the basics. We secure the crime scenes. This was a very serious crime and was treated as such. A team was quickly assembled and all parts of the organisation swung into place: the forensic element, the search teams, internal communications. Information was circulated to officers throughout the force and an investigation team was established here in North Queen Street with a hand-picked team of senior detectives.

Retired officer John Horan also stresses the importance of finding forensic traces, cautioning however that nowadays most criminals are very much aware of methods to help avoid detection:

> Any good organised crime group now are very, very forensically conscious. But no matter how careful you are, there is always a strong possibility that you will leave a trace, and forensic science is increasing in sophistication every day. That's one key element of the investigation.

Det. Supt Sproule would confirm:

> The terrorists involved were very forensically aware. Floors were mopped, surfaces rubbed down with cleaner and bleach and so on, cups, glasses, anything that could have been touched by these individuals was taken away with them. Police held the house for at least a week to ensure that all possible painstaking examinations were carried out. We could not afford to rush that sort of thing, which meant that the families were out of their houses at Christmas. That was a decision we took reluctantly, but we didn't want to miss any vital evidence.

Aside from the forensic evidence-gathering, the detectives would be taking other measures, well away from the public gaze, to try to unravel the puzzle of the robbery. As John Horan explained:

> The second very strong line the investigators will take is to 'shake the trees', so to speak. They will make contact with every informer that works within the Northern Ireland environment to see what they can throw up. Not only have these particular crooks got a very good haul, but it will be a very good payday for any informant who can come up with sufficient information to lead to recovery and arrests.

A third crucial aspect of the police investigation would focus quickly on the practicalities of uncovering circumstantial evidence. John Horan explained:

> Bank accounts will be very strictly monitored now. The National Criminal Intelligence Service are already probably very deeply involved in checking bank accounts, not just here in Northern Ireland but throughout the UK. The Garda Siochána Financial Investigation Unit will be heavily involved too. Throughout Europe there is a very, very good investigative interconnection in white collar crime, although this robbery of course is not white collar crime—but all those

financial investigation teams will also be collaborating, so there will be a worldwide approach to it.

Det. Supt Sproule tasked a number of officers to try to trace the van. It was an extensive search for clues.

We have carried out hundreds of enquiries in this regard. We still are not sure of the origin of the particular van that was used. As you probably know, it was bearing 'ringer' plates. The original van was locked up in another part of the city at the time of the crime. It's an important line of enquiry. The vehicle used was a very distinctive one. There's a distinctive tail lift and the cab has two lights on the roof. It's not the normal type of vehicle.

We're also pursuing reports that the van's origins might be tracked to Wales. Only a limited number of these particular vans were manufactured. One similar vehicle was stolen in Wales about a month prior to the robbery. We still haven't located it and it's a very important line of enquiry.

From the outset of their investigation the police were under extreme pressure to get a good result quickly. The force has come in for serious criticism about its failure to get even a 'sniff' of the robbery plans. According to John Horan, the criminal gang involved was acutely aware of considerations such as its own security and as such avoided the risk of information about their plans being leaked by reducing the details of the raid to only a few on a 'need-to-know' basis:

I would imagine that it was very tightly controlled, intelligence-wise. They kept the actual knowledge of what was to happen to a very small amount of people. The actual organisation might be large but I would say there were only a few key members who knew exactly what they were going to do.

Commenting on the apparent failure of police intelligence to gain advance warning of the raid, Det. Supt Sproule remarked:

No, unfortunately we had no intelligence of the raid in this case. It would be a luxury for all police forces to have prior knowledge of all types of serious crime. This was a highly professional, highly organised crime carried out by ruthless terrorists. They keep a very tight cell and only those people who are involved and need to know are told of actually what is going on. Such a set-up is not something that's easily penetrated, but we as an organisation are working very hard at getting intelligence, and, more importantly, evidence that we can place before the courts. This raid was similar to a number of other robberies we believe were carried out by the same organisation: the same modus operandi and the same operatives, we believe, were involved. It would be a mixture of individuals, as there are many facets to this type of an operation—the intelligence gatherers, the planners, the people who physically carry out the crime involved, the people who subsequently deal with the amount of money that was taken.

While Det. Supt Sproule stopped short of revealing the identities of the gang the police suspected was involved, several other police officers were less reticent about the list of suspects. The chief suspect they have named is Bobby Storey, a dedicated republican leader of some repute. From west Belfast, Storey is acknowledged as a determined and ruthless leader of men: someone with the necessary leadership qualities to organise the great IRA Maze Prison escape of 1983. Storey, who became the IRA's director of intelligence in 2003, was named in Parliament after the raid as the IRA's most senior intelligence officer, the orchestrator of the robbery and a loyal supporter of the Sinn Féin leadership's peace strategy. He is also a close associate of Gerry Adams.

Police believe that Storey was the 'brains' of the operation to raid Special Branch offices at Castlereagh in 2002, when confidential intelligence files were stolen, which resulted in many police officers and others outside the force being compelled to move home for security reasons. In 1999 the Special Branch believed Storey was in charge of a group of what they referred to as 'white-collar IRA spies' responsible for gathering intelligence on judges, senior police officers, senior civil servants and barristers involved in prosecuting terrorist cases for the Director of Public Prosections. The spy-ring was discovered during the police investigation of the 1996 IRA bomb attack on the British Army's Northern Ireland headquarters at Thiepval Barracks in Lisburn, Co. Antrim. Computer discs found in a west Belfast community centre revealed details of the IRA's intelligence gathering operation. Storey was arrested and charged with possessing information that could be of use to terrorists. But the case collapsed on a legal technicality.

Police also suspect Storey of involvement in a number of other so-called 'tiger' robberies, which involved cash being obtained after hostages are used to gain access to safes. It is thought the Northern Bank raid was the forty-first 'tiger' robbery in Northern Ireland since 2003. Police believe the IRA was responsible for a number of these robberies, namely:

- *May 2004*: Cigarettes, alcohol and electrical goods worth over £1m were stolen in a robbery at a Makro store in south Belfast. At the time, the police said an experienced professional gang of seven individuals used a 40-foot lorry to make off with the goods.

- *August 2004*: A bank in Strabane, Co. Tyrone, was robbed of £500,000 when a group of armed men broke into a house and held a bank official's family hostage overnight. The bank employee was taken to the bank the next morning and ordered to hand over the cash. The family was then released unharmed. Initially, the INLA was thought to be responsible but then the PSNI said it was the work of the IRA.

- *October 2004*: In the Ardoyne area of north Belfast, a family was held hostage while an IRA gang robbed Gallaghers' cigarette factory, escaping with £2m worth of cigarettes. A member of the family was forced to open the warehouse in an industrial estate a few miles away from Ardoyne.

Police believe key members of this IRA team of robbers were also involved in the Northern Bank robbery.

According to reporter John Cassidy of the *Sunday World*, the IRA had recruited a convicted criminal to help them carry out the biggest bank raid in British history. In September 2005, Cassidy named the individual when he wrote:

> Brendan McIlkearney has been rewarded for his skills by being appointed second-in-command to the IRA's head of intelligence Bobby Storey. The *Sunday World* has learned that McIlkearney was recruited into the IRA ranks within the past two years as an adviser on how to pull off robberies. He was a well-known criminal who for years had been part of a gang of crooks and bank robbers led by convicted armed robber Cecil Walsh. IRA sources described McIlkearney, who hails from the Grosvenor Road area of west Belfast, as a 'ceasefire soldier', only recruited into the ranks to help pull off spectacular robberies. 'He never fired one shot for the Republican movement, yet he is now Bobby Storey's number two,' said one disgruntled IRA member. 'People have done 20 years in the IRA and haven't got to where he has in such a short space of time.'
>
> Over the past year or more, the IRA has pulled off five massive robberies right across Northern Ireland from Belfast to Tyrone. And not a single person has been charged by the PSNI in connection with any of the heists.

Cassidy went on to say that 'tiger kidnappings' had become a useful tool for the IRA. And he pointed out that the same method had been used successfully by Cecil Walsh's criminal gang. Quoting republican sources, Cassidy further describes how Storey and McIlkearney are regularly seen together on the Falls Road in Belfast.

As a result of publishing this story, Cassidy received death threats from the IRA. News of the threats were brought to his attention by the PSNI.

Of course, by then the police had already gone public to say they believed the IRA was behind the Northern Bank robbery. It was in January 2005, less than a month after the robbery, that the Chief Constable of the PSNI—Hugh Orde—openly and publicly accused the Provisionals of the crime. Having briefed the chairman of the Policing Board, Sir Desmond Rea, and his deputy, Dennis Bradley, the Chief Constable told reporters: 'In my opinion the Provisional IRA were responsible for this crime and all main lines of inquiry currently being undertaken are in that direction.'

Where the Chief Constable had gone, the Independent Monitoring Commission (IMC)—set up by both the Irish and British governments to monitor the activities of paramilitary groups during the ceasefires—was soon to follow. In February 2005, the IMC clearly laid the blame for the Northern Bank raid at the door of the IRA. It also blamed the organisation for the robbery at the Makro store in Dunmurry in May, the abduction of hostages and the robbery of the Iceland store in Strabane in September, and the kidnap and robbery of individuals during the £2m cigarette robbery in Belfast in October.

Searches carried out by the police in Belfast soon after the robbery gave an early indication of where the police thought the blame lay. Within days of starting his investigation, Det. Supt Sproule sought search warrants for a number of business premises, as well as property used by community groups in west Belfast. The police believed the stolen cash had been taken to a location not far from the bank for distribution to south Armagh and Louth in other vehicles. Given that the van used in the raid made two visits to the bank one hour apart, the police tried to work out on a map how far the van could have travelled after its first trip to the bank.

They also raided the homes of a number of prominent republicans—one of whom was the adjutant of the Belfast Brigade and a relative and friend of Gerry Adams. They also searched the homes of John Trainor, the IRA intelligence officer of the Belfast Brigade, and Eddie Copeland, a senior north Belfast republican: here they removed Christmas presents from under the family Christmas tree along with a large number of Copeland's pairs of shoes.

Asked whether these raids were based on information or were being used as a means of flushing out the robbers, this is what Det. Supt Andy Sproule had to say:

The crime at the bank was a raid. Police carry out searches which are lawfully authorised. A senior officer must authorise the conducting of a search. Police conducted searches, intelligence led-searches, at a number of houses where we suspected individuals living there had been involved in the crime. A large amount of property was seized and is currently being examined. This is a lengthy task. Some of the scientific processes that are used take an extremely long time. We won't be rushed in this investigation so that any potential evidence could be lost. What we want to do is ensure that all the evidence that we can possibly find is there. I'm sure in the course of time there will be arrests but not at this stage and we won't be rushed into any precipitive action that could jeopardise future court proceedings.

Early on in the investigation, the police had to consult with Ward and McMullan to try to establish exactly how much cash had been removed from the vaults. The bank also brought in a team to quickly carry out an audit to help police get a clear idea of what exactly was missing. The Northern Bank's Deputy Chief Executive Colin Dundas was presented for an interview for the UTV *Insight* programme days after the robbery. He told me:

Interestingly, there were various speculations about the amount of money stolen being circulated on the morning after the robbery. There were a number of figures in the media —up to forty million pounds, in fact. A figure at that stage of approximately £22m was disclosed to us, based on the information we had at a time when we were still dealing with the crime scene. Over the next few days we got into the cash centre, spoke with our staff, reviewed the CCTV footage and were able to clarify a figure of £26.5m. A third party then came in to do an independent review which confirmed this figure.

That internal audit also provided the police with a breakdown of the various denominations of notes that were taken. Det. Supt Sproule explained:

I can say that there's at least sixteen and a half million pounds for which we have the serial numbers: new Northern Bank twenty pound and ten pound notes. The serial numbers have now been widely circulated throughout the world so these notes will be difficult to get into the banking system. But there is at least ten million pounds which is untraceable, for which we don't have serial numbers, and we don't know whether that is starting to filter into the banking system as yet.

So even if the robbers were going to have difficulty laundering the £16m in new notes, they still had a handsome payday with £10m in used and untraceable notes. The actual breakdown of the stolen notes is as follows:

- £1.15m in new Northern Bank £100 and £50 notes: serial numbers unknown
- £9m in new Northern Bank £20 notes
- £7.5m in new Northern Bank £10 notes
- £8.85m in used notes of which £4.4m were used Northern Bank £20 notes: the remainder made up of Bank of Ireland, First Trust, Bank of England and other notes.

John Horan specialised as a financial investigator in the RUC and PSNI before his retirement. In fact, he was known during his career as a money laundering 'anorak'. He has talked at length about the methods the Northern Bank gang might try to use to launder £26.5m:

Bizarrely, the fact that they have stolen so much money is going to make it very, very difficult for them to launder. And so, if I was still on the investigation side, I would be very happy, because the money has to pop to the surface somewhere. Immediately it does, the dedicated financial investigators still working within PSNI and within the National Criminal Intelligence Service will make strenuous efforts to track it down. In fact, every law enforcement agency from the Revenue upwards will be aware of what's going on, including the Assets Recovery Agency.

These bodies will be looking for unusual deposits, strange bank accounts being opened, property being bought, high value goods being purchased, changes in the lifestyles of non-criminals. All of these are indications that there's more money in the market place.

In fact, it's not because the police have the serial numbers of all the new notes which will make these difficult for the robbers to launder—it's the sheer volume of money that's been taken which is going to cause them most difficulty. Although it has to be said that the criminals must have been aware that the police would very quickly find out that they had sequentially numbered notes, but I think that when they got the opportunity to take the money they simply took it and didn't think it through.

The used notes they stole, which amount, according to the figures issued by the police and the bank, to at least ten million pounds, would be only marginally less difficult for them to deal with, in fact. You're going to have to break this money up. You're going to have to do what's known in money laundering terms as 'smurfing it'—breaking it down into smaller and smaller amounts so you can get it deposited without attracting undue attention. Now, that's alright if you're working with an amount like, say, £100,000. In that case, you pick fifty little criminals and give them £2,000 each and you then set them up to open their bank accounts and to do whatever you want. You still have control over the £100,000. Multiply that to 26 million and it becomes an astronomical problem for the robbers. To 'smurf' that sum of money is going to be extremely difficult, and to move it in large amounts is going to be equally problematic.

There is no de minimis in Ireland—that is, no threshold as to how much money you can open an account with in cash terms without alerting the authorities. De minimis thresholds are in existence in America and Australia, where banks must report sums of money over a certain amount. I think in America it's 10,000 US dollars. Now, in that scenario, all the criminals need to do is 'smurf' it in batches of $9,999. When the legislation was written for the United Kingdom, the authorities decided to do without a de minimis because by introducing one, all they were doing was ensuring that the criminals stayed underneath the limit, with no one having any obligation to report it. It was reckoned that if there is no de minimis, anything in the least suspicious, involving even small sums, will be reported.

As for the old, the used notes that the robbers stole, they would attempt to get rid of these through the normal outlets: bent public houses, bent clubs, or whatever—places criminals frequent and where there is a cash economy in place, and these could be anywhere in the UK or in the South. So they start to drip-feed it into the economy that way. Again, in this case, that's going to be extremely difficult because of the sheer volume of cash.

The bank and the police consulted about the best ways of making it even more difficult for the robbers to launder the cash. The result was the decision to withdraw all of the bank's existing notes and re-issue Northern Bank notes with a new design. Colin Dundas explained the thinking:

> There were two main drivers behind this decision. The first was to maintain the public's confidence in the integrity of Northern Bank's notes and to make sure that people are comfortable when they receive and handle our notes. The second reason was to assist the authorities in making sure that the people who took the money don't get value for it.

With a print order for £300m worth of new notes, there was inevitably a time delay in getting the notes into the public domain. The whole undertaking was naturally an enormous challenge for the bank's management.

According to John Horan, a definitive cut-off date by which the old notes could be presented to the bank for exchange was an important part of the strategy to withdraw the old notes from circulation:

It will shorten the period of time available to the gang to launder the money. It pushes them into a scenario where they have to move a lot faster than they would probably like to. The best case scenario for this particular gang would be to be able to keep the money long-term. We're talking twelve months, fifteen months. To let the heat go out of the situation and then start laundering the money. By withdrawing their notes, the Northern Bank have forced the hands of the criminals: they must get rid of the stolen notes straight away.

Of course, a by-product of the move to withdraw the old notes is that there will be an awful lot of other crime groups who have cash in Northern Bank notes and they're going to have to get rid of theirs as well—so there's going to be a flurry of activity from those needing to dispense with the notes— including from people who are evading tax. We have already seen this scenario in Craigavon and Portadown where a large sum of money was taken into a bank to be deposited for exactly these reasons. The people depositing the money had panicked and decided they had to get rid of it and of course that caused interest within the law enforcement community. As I said, all our contacts will be out now with the financial institutions and they will be looking for this money to surface or any money like it.

But Horan did not completely agree with Chief Constable Hugh Orde's assessment of the situation, that because of the issue of new Northern Bank notes, 'in essence, this large robbery has become the largest theft of wastepaper in the living history of Northern Ireland'. Horan's view was less positive:

I don't accept that. All it has changed is the time-frame within which the robbers must get rid of the money. If they can manage to get it into the system without being detected before the new notes come in, they've laundered it. It's successful.

But the note re-issue was an important and tangible manoeuvre for a bank that had so comprehensively been out-manoeuvred by a gang of determined robbers. For a few brief moments it helped the Northern Bank to restore something of its lost pride.

Behind the scenes, however, the bank and the police were busy trying to figure out who was acting as the 'mole' for the robbers. All forty members of staff at the cash centre fell under suspicion. Management decided it was essential to re-deploy each and every one of these individuals, but, according to Colin Dundas, this was not due to the fact that employees were under suspicion:

> The decision to move the staff out of the cash centre has nothing to do with suspicions, it's to do with staff welfare. The criminals had a significant amount of information on the individuals and their families. We have no way of knowing if that was restricted to the two individuals who unfortunately were involved, but given that the key-holding rota could have involved anyone, we have to presume a worst-case scenario, where details are being held on more people working in the cash centre.

Dundas believes the bank was capable of making this drastic step without damaging the morale of staff at the cash centre. 'It will be done in a sensitive way. It will be done on a one-to-one basis in terms of finding suitable jobs for each individual in other parts of the organisation, but I think there's a management responsibility for the welfare of staff, and the right thing to do is to move our staff out of the cash centre.'

However, no amount of spin from the Northern Bank could detract from the fact that staff felt isolated and 'dirty' because of the way they were treated in the aftermath of the robbery. As one of them confided: 'Bank security failed big-time and we were being made the scapegoats for the robbery. They should be looking at the management who allowed this to happen—not blaming staff at our level.'

Colin Dundas is quick to accept that the bank's security measures failed:

> Our security procedures on the day did not stand up to the

challenge that we were faced with. Inevitably, the cash held in the cash centre must be accessible. Every hour of every day, and particularly in the busy Christmas period, we're getting deliveries into the cash centre, we're getting funds coming in from other branches, from large retailers, and we're dispensing cash out of it. So accessibility is key.

Now, the controls around that accessibility are typical human controls. They have to be. But here, those human controls broke down—there was no way of safeguarding against that.

And it's the human factor that means it is so difficult for banks to secure themselves, the human element which makes for weakness on a number of fronts. Jonty Brown and John Horan have all too often investigated crimes made possible by the exploitation of this 'human factor'. Brown told me:

If you're talking about inside involvement, where people are blackmailed and their families are held hostage, well, once you've got someone, a bank staff member and their families are held, then they will disarm alarms. There are no alarms that can't be overridden when you've got the people who hold the keys to those alarms.

Any security system, no matter how sophisticated, no matter what provisions are in place, is only as good as the human element and once the bandits have got control of that human element, then there are no procedures that can't be breached, and this robbery is the classic example of that.

John Horan identified a number of measures the banks could take to protect themselves against this type of robbery:

The first thing is to ensure that the staff working in that environment are at a sufficiently high level. Secondly, staff should be educated in the very good anti-kidnap procedures which are generally in place, and which have been agreed between the banks and the police. But at the end of the day, let's be brutally frank about it, money's only paper. When it's affecting human lives, that's got to be your prime concern and that is the police's prime concern in these investigations and they're very good at it. I mean they take a very measured approach to any investigation where a kidnapping has taken place.

But according to Colin Dundas, his bank staff were and are regularly given training in anti-kidnap measures adopted by the bank in conjunction with the police. He stated, in fact, that Chris Ward and Kevin McMullan had only just finished a training course a few weeks prior to the robbery:

All we can do is see how we can minimise the impact of this kind of risk in the future. I don't think, however, you can make the risk go away as long as there are people out there who are prepared to go to those lengths to get at the bank's cash.

This is not a new format in terms of robbery. It's been going on for a period of time in banks across Northern Ireland. If there was a simple way to stop it, the banks would have found it by now.

Our staff are given training: awareness training and kidnap training. The aspect of these situations that you can't simulate is the real-life trauma of being put into such a position. There is training in place, but realistically nobody can sit with hindsight and say, 'You should have acted differently in a situation like that'. The best training in the world still can't reduce the stress of a gun being held to your head and going to work not knowing whether you'll ever see your family again. If you are asked to make the call between the security of your family and the security of the bank's cash, it's a very straightforward one to make and I don't think anybody would level any criticism at the individuals involved.

Of course, what happened in the robbery of the Northern Bank in Belfast is not the first time such a kidnapping had been experienced by the bank's owners, National Australia Bank. The Australians had come to Ireland in 1987 when they bought the Northern Bank. They established the National Irish Bank in the Republic to operate the Northern Bank branches there as a separate entity. In 1993 the notorious Dublin criminal Martin Cahill, known as the General, abducted the head of the bank's operations in the South, as *Sunday Independent* crime reporter Jim Cusack recounted to me:

> A robbery like this happened in Dublin thirteen years ago. Jim Lacey, head of the National Irish Bank—the head of the bank—was kidnapped and held hostage, while his wife and children were taken away, and since that time banks here have set up internal CCTV monitoring systems on their premises that are controlled from outside the bank, with no one in the bank knowing where they are. Even if the Chief Executive goes into a bank vault here and says 'open it up', he'll get a call from this independent monitoring station. It's one of the systems that I gather didn't exist in the Northern Bank.

The Northern Bank robbery highlighted the whole issue of bank security and, according to Det. Supt Andy Sproule, it's an issue that was discussed at the highest level:

> I know that the Organised Crime Task Force and the Security Minister met with all four banks to discuss the implications of this robbery for bank security. Clearly all was not as it should have been. I think probably with that you have to take into account the human aspect of the situation. Two families were held hostage by ruthless terrorists: guns and knives were produced. The families were traumatised, terrified, and they did what they were told because they simply had no other choice. That's something that you can't legislate for and these people were left in an invidious position. No amount of training or procedures can balance the fear and the trauma experienced by those poor families.

The Northern Bank's security review focused on a number of areas, most crucially:

- CCTV cameras
- Human weaknesses
- False economies on security systems and procedures

Hugh Conkey worked as a bank messenger (a porter in uniform) in the Northern Bank headquarters for eighteen years, mostly in charge of running the day-to-day security arrangements. He is convinced that in his time security would have detected the robbery: 'Such a thing would never have happened with the procedures that we had in place. For example, anybody walking out the staff door with any bag, it would have mattered what was in it . . . Their bags would have been searched and they might have had a body search as well before they would have gone out the door.'

But Conkey would not be more specific about how the robbery could and should have been prevented: 'I'm not going to disclose any details about the systems presently in place, but with the systems maintained by my men, myself and certainly the previous Chief Executives, it would never, ever have happened.'

And the robbery couldn't have happened at a worse time in the bank's history—coming as it did a matter of weeks after its owners had agreed to sell it. As Christmas 2004 approached, the Australians were preparing to move out and the new Danish owners were preparing to move in.

National Australia Bank had struck a deal with Danish bank Danske which would see the Danes taking over the Northern Bank and its southern sister bank, National Irish Bank, in March 2005.

Now this most unwanted Christmas 'gift' prompted questions about the bank's security systems.

The Northern Bank had once controlled all its own security. That's how it worked in Hugh Conkey's day. But when the National Australia Bank became the new owners in 1987, a decision was made to sub-contract such security duties to an outside company.

Hugh Conkey, who retired after the decision to subcontract was made, said he had spoken at one point with a senior official of the new security company: 'Off the cuff, he told me in his own words, and I quote: "I have to engineer it to save £100,000 per year for the next five years," and I said to myself, Well, you'll have a job on your hands.'

As far as Hugh Conkey was concerned, the cutbacks were purely a money-saving exercise. I asked Colin Dundas about this change in security arrangements.

AUTHOR: And what did this company promise you in terms of the cash unit?
DUNDAS: I mean I'm not getting into the details of our contract with the company.
AUTHOR: Did they promise you that they would give you savings of £300,000 a year for three years?
DUNDAS: I don't have the detail of that and I wouldn't comment on that. That's a commercial arrangement between ourselves and the outsource supplier.
AUTHOR: Isn't the truth of the matter though that you were trying to get security on the cheap?
DUNDAS: There are a number of issues when you make an outsourcing decision. First and foremost on any of these is that the level of service is what you need it to be, and we would not have compromised on that in terms of the original thinking behind the decision to outsource any security.
AUTHOR: It hasn't done you much good, the savings, whatever savings you made?
DUNDAS: No one should prejudge what the outcome of the review will say. The only thing that went wrong here was that people put guns to our staff members' heads.

But if it is true that the huge savings made on security in any way contributed to the success of the IRA's robbery plans, then the management of the National Australia Bank stands accused of killing the 'cash cow' that had saved their hides.

As we will see, there was an imperative for the IRA to rob the bank when it did—and it had nothing to do with the political landscape but was all about their ability to exploit a bank that was in so many ways ripe for robbery.

04 | ACT OF BETRAYAL

'The net effect of these changes would have been the means of preventing the robbery because without the ability to over-ride the internal security doors, the robbers' plans could easily have been frustrated.'—NORTHERN BANK SOURCE, 'RICHARD'

—

It was now or never. That was the blunt message delivered from the Northern Bank 'insider' to the IRA robbery gang. The 'insider' knew some detail of the plan to rob the bank. After all, the robbery gang had relied on the 'insider' for details to help plot the raid.

But as a trusted employee of the bank, that person had also become aware of plans to change security that could potentially wreck the detailed operation to relieve the bank's vaults of cash.

The bank's head of security had devised a new system of controlling the keys to the bank's treasures in the basement of Northern Bank headquarters in Belfast. If the robbers did not move swiftly, all their preparations over the past two years to steal from the cash centre would have been time wasted. And time was now of the essence.

The proposed changes would drastically alter the system of operation inside the bank in relation to the keys and how they were used by the designated key-holders—the cash centre supervisors. The intention was to relieve the pressure on the supervisors by passing control of their master keys to the vault to security staff.

The 'insider' also informed his contact in the robbery gang that the bank had been a little slow in moving on the orders sent down from above. This delay provided vital time to proceed with the planned raid. It was, in essence, a delay that gave the raiders a lucky 'second chance' to go ahead. But the 'insider' warned the gang that soon the changes would be implemented and that could potentially be disastrous for their plan.

It was Friday 17 December 2004. In an office at Northern Bank headquarters, the bank's security company—Maybins—finally came face-to-face with senior management at the cash centre to discuss the directive from the bank's head of security. The directive had been issued just over three weeks previously. And normally when the bank's head of security issues an order, it is anticipated that it will be acted upon immediately.

But according to my bank source, let's call him Richard as he's someone who wishes to remain anonymous, there had been a number of attempts in the weeks before 17 December to arrange this crucial get-together. That the meeting did not take place, according to Richard, was down to difficulties presented from within the cash centre. 'I think two dates were set,' he recalled, 'but certainly one of the meetings was cancelled at fairly short notice because it did not suit someone within the cash centre. The other meeting was also postponed and again I think that was for similar reasons, although I cannot be one hundred per cent on that.'

One of those meetings was certainly arranged to take place two weeks before the crucial meeting eventually took place on 17 December. Those expected to attend were the cash centre manager, the cash centre deputy manager, supervisors at the cash centre and representatives of Maybins.

When that meeting was cancelled by someone on the staff at Northern Bank headquarters, it was re-scheduled for Friday 17 December.

What happened at the meeting on 17 December is not only interesting, but provides many points worthy of attention by the police officers investigating the robbery. In attendance were the deputy manager of the cash centre, two supervisors—one of whom was Kevin McMullan—and the Maybins representative.

Discussion centred on the directive from the bank's head of security which would have the effect of changing the working practice of those supervisors in the cash centre who had access to the keys to the vaults. My source explained:

> The supervisors—that is the key-holders to the vault—had the run of the cash centre. They could use their keys to override the internal security doors. So instead of having to wait while they buzzed up to security staff in the control room for access in and out of the two sets of doors leading from the cash office to the bullion bay, they could simply use their keys.
>
> These were master keys and gave them total access to everything in the cash centre. That obviously meant that they could let themselves in and out of the cash centre. Not only through the security doors I have referred to, but also by another door at the top of a spiral staircase leading to the floor above and the staff exit.
>
> But now the head of security wanted that facility removed. No longer would the supervisors hold the master keys that gave them total freedom to move around inside the cash centre. The change would mean that only by buzzing security staff could the sterile set of doors be unlocked and locked. The supervisors would be compelled to hand in their keys and with that obviously a major part of their security status.
>
> Once the new arrangements came into place, the keys of the cash centre would be held in the control room, and in order to get through the security doors (interlocking doors), staff would have had to rely on the security staff in the control room to open and close the doors for them.

This truly was a 'key' impediment to the guaranteed success of the robbery plan.

During the meeting on 17 December, it was decided that the change in arrangements could not be implemented immediately but would be put in place by the end of business on the following Monday—20 December.

The suggestion was that it was too late in the day to have supervisors hand in the master keys. Monday would make more sense and be more convenient.

This decision was arrived at after some considerable discussion. And it is my understanding that it was Kevin McMullan who undertook to introduce the new arrangements to everyone on the Monday and to begin the process of implementation.

Once the decision to change the arrangements for the Monday was taken, the other supervisor present at the meeting declared that he should be excused from any further discussion as he had just agreed to a swap in his shift, which meant that he was no longer going to be on duty with Kevin McMullan on the Monday.

'He had changed shifts with Chris Ward at Chris Ward's request and so Chris Ward was brought into the meeting,' Richard told me, adding: 'The net effect of these changes in security would have been the means of preventing the robbery, because without the ability to over-ride the internal security doors, the robbers' plans could so easily have been frustrated.'

In short, the timing of the IRA robbery of the bank appears to have been determined by proposed internal security changes within the Northern Bank's cash centre rather than the widely speculated view that it was linked to the breakdown in finding a political settlement.

The imperative was to rob the bank before it became impossible, rather than to make—as many commentators suggested—some kind of 'spectacular' statement about the political deadlock in the same way as the Canary Wharf bomb in London in 1996.

The issue for the robbers—on advice from the 'insider'—was to carry out the raid whilst the supervisors had keys that could over-ride the security doors internally and at the very least get a cargo of cash up to the bullion bay area without alerting security staff in the control room. That way they could get the cash out of the most secure area and into the bullion bay—just one door away from the street. And once behind the door on to the street, it would be more easily prised out of the building by, for example, armed men.

'Clearly the gang knew they could force their way in through the street door at the bullion bay if necessary,' said Richard, 'and they could have used guns to achieve that. So it was vital to the

gang that at the very least the two supervisors could use their keys
to get in and out through the internal sterile area created by the
two sets of doors leading up to the bullion bay.

'The supervisors, already under extreme duress, would not be
dependent on security staff to breach the most important
security doors from the vault to the street. But if the robbery had
taken place twenty-four hours later, the supervisors would no
longer have the capability to over-ride those internal security
doors. And the raiders could not afford to take that chance.'

As it happened, according to Chris Ward in an interview with
the *Irish News* and with the BBC *Spotlight* programme, he and
Kevin did buzz the security staff in the control room to get the
doors opened so they could get the money from the vaults to the
bullion bay area after first alerting security staff to the fact, as
instructed by the robbers, that they were bringing up trolleys of
rubbish to be collected by the waste company used by the bank.
They made four runs in all with crates of new notes packed in
green boxes for collection on the gang's first trip to the bank.
What Ward and McMullan had delivered up to the bullion bay
was £15m worth of new notes that had only been delivered to the
bank that very morning.

This is how Chris Ward described this part of the robbery
when speaking to BBC reporter Kevin Magee:

> So what Kevin and I had to do was get these green boxes and
> just put them on trolleys, bring them up a lift and bring them
> through two security doors which are controlled by the
> control room.
>
> So we had to buzz in and say, you know, 'you have to let us
> out of this door and then you have to let us out at the next
> door,' and what Kevin had to do was phone the control room
> and, under the instructions obviously of the gang, he was to
> tell the control room that there was a company coming in to
> collect rubbish from us from the cash centre and that Kevin
> and myself would be bringing old boxes and rubbish and bags
> and stuff for these guys to collect.
>
> So then the control room expected us to come through all

these, because they have to let us through these interlocked doors, so when we came up with all the first crates, which we were saying were rubbish, we buzzed the control room and they let us through the various doors and we left it at the big gate, just at the big gate, so as soon as you opened the gate the stuff was sitting there, and we had to do that four times, up and down four times.

Ward then explained to the reporter that the cash was now safely out of the vault but was not yet outside the bank premises:

What's keeping the money from the street is the gate. So what actually happened was we had to do it four times, so there you have all your green boxes sitting there with all your new notes, rubbish round it and me and Kevin standing there, so what I then had to do was—because of my last phone call I was instructed to do this—was come out of the bank, go out to the street, phone these people.

Ward had to let the gang know the money was ready for collection. And remember, the gang made it clear to the two bank staff that they would not be entering the premises.

So on the morning after the IRA removed over £26m, bank executives must have been kicking themselves over the failure to implement the changes earlier that might, just might, have saved the day.

Two days after the robbery, the National Irish Bank Chief Executive came to Belfast to head a meeting to discuss the robbery. As part of their knee-jerk reaction, the bank insisted that the site security manager had to be let go along with two other security staff—all employed by Maybins.

It was possible for the bank to dictate who should be sacked under the terms of the contract in what is known as 'third party pressure'. It gives the bank the right to veto any employee it feels is not suitable—i.e. someone employed by the third party.

At the time Maybins felt certain they would become the fall guys for the security failure. In the months immediately prior to the robbery, the company had been trying to secure their contract, which was up for renewal. In fact, it should have been signed for another three years in November. But, according to Richard, things had dragged on . . . and on . . . and in spite of repeated requests for the matter to be resolved, the bank did not respond.

Given that National Australia Bank had sold the Northern Bank and National Irish Bank to Danish bank Danske, it is perhaps understandable that a three-year contract binding the new owners to the existing security operation would not have been signed.

After all, the new owners were due to take possession in March and, in any event, the Northern Bank had no ability to buy the security contract. It found that it did not have a purchasing department since for the past seventeen years all purchases had been handled by the National Australia Bank's purchasing office.

So, Maybins were told by the Northern Bank that they would have to accept a rolling contract on a year-to-year basis until the new owners took possession and made their own decisions.

Understandably, Maybins are just a little anxious about the future, although I am given to understand that aside from the removal of three security staff from the Northern Bank contract, Maybins has had its workload increased as a result of changes implemented following the raid.

Maybins believes it can defend its position in the aftermath of the robbery. Its main responsibility was to secure the bank from any outside attempts to breach security and while it was looking outwards, it felt that the bank had a responsibility to look inwardly at its own staff.

Maybins did not speak publicly after the robbery. But I know the bank's kidnap security measures did not reach the necessary requirements. Richard told me:

> The bank and all its security advisers were obviously aware of the kidnap threat. It had been used in various attacks on branches throughout the country but no one ever thought about the prospect of *two* members of staff being taken hostage.

The measures were of course considered adequate for what was perceived as the threat—but no one thought outside the box and no one contemplated the scenario which proved to be the bank's undoing . . . i.e. the kidnapping of two families.

Another bank source told me:

The dual key system was devised to frustrate kidnappings. The bank felt this was a sound policy in that it would be difficult enough for kidnappers to research enough details on one bank employee. And if they did manage to do that, then the individual concerned would have to explain to them that his or her keys alone could not open the vault. Up until this robbery, the bank regarded the dual key system as foolproof. It was considered good practice. Especially when the bank considered that the rolling rota system could permeate any number of combinations when it was devising the 'pairs' who would be on duty at any particular time.

So for the criminals to breach that security was something the bank had not envisaged. It shook them and their complacency. It meant the gang had to know the names of the people who had key-holding responsibilities; they had to know when their two targets would be on duty; they had to know the movements of their targets—their home addresses, their car registrations, etc.—in order to execute the simultaneous kidnappings.

But when the National Irish Bank Chief Executive came to Belfast for the meeting to review security two days after the Northern Bank's name had been dragged on to the front page of virtually every newspaper in the Western world, the company had more to concern itself with than attaching blame to Maybins' security operation.

There were many questions they needed to find answers to if this was to be avoided again in the future. The new owners would want an explanation and would expect stringent measures to be adopted to avoid any repeat of what was not only a political hot potato but also a profoundly embarrassing episode for the bank to endure.

The bank's credibility had been undermined and so that initial meeting to review security procedures had lots to discuss, not least of which were the following:

- Who was working for the gang from the inside?
- Why did security not notice something out of the ordinary was taking place?
- Where did our kidnap procedures go wrong?
- Why was Chris Ward able to walk out with over £1m in a sports bag?
- Why could security not see what was going on in the cash centre?
- Did we have sufficient security staff on duty in the first place?
- Were our closed circuit television cameras adequate for the job?
- In making savings on security provision, had the bank exposed itself to greater risk?
- Should we offer a reward for information?

It was certainly a time for some soul-searching about security procedures. Obviously the police investigation was paramount and the bank would do everything it could to co-operate with the investigating officers, whilst at the same time trying to repair the damage done to its own credibility, and make sure it understood exactly how this had been allowed to happen from its own security viewpoint.

According to Jonty Brown, it's at times like this that the victims of such a crime consider offering a reward for information leading to a conviction. It had worked for him many times before:

As I said before, vital to this scenario would be an informant, and it amazes me that a substantial award wasn't offered immediately this robbery happened because against £26m, one million or two million pounds would have oiled a lot of wheels.

A lot of people would be disaffected with republican paramilitaries where they wouldn't normally come forward to police, if you have a tab like two million pounds or one million pounds . . .

And you can tell them if they're ringing in to ask how do we get it, if they knew all it takes is one relative. All it takes is one person, that one weak link, to ring in and say: I know where it is.

Brown used the enticement of rewards in the past when heading the Robbery Squad, but it was also something that was considered by the CID:

We had people coming forward from the oddest of areas, where for instance they were maybe washing dishes looking out a window and seeing a van leaving a garage. That person maybe knows that there is a 10 per cent reward available of the £1m worth of stolen goods, and rings into us and says: 'This could be part of your consignment'. She had seen these suits being brought out and yes we got all the suits back, every suit, a million pounds worth of suits taken in that robbery, we got them back.

We got them back because there was a reward offered to the general public and one lady miles from the robbery saw untoward activity and rang in. A million pounds would have oiled those wheels. A million pounds reward, and in this case it could be two million pounds because there's a substantial amount of money. It would also have saved them having to change the notes. I'm not saying that it would have worked. It *could* have worked. It surprises me that it wasn't offered.

That sentiment was shared by John Horan:

That does surprise me but I'm sure there will be an inevitable reward posted . . . but the police initially will trawl their existing informants and the rewards, of course, will be correspondingly large for anybody that can provide information.

In the days after the robbery I asked the police about the situation regarding a reward and was told by Det. Supt Sproule:

> Well, there are many mechanisms in place to reward information . . . through Crime Stoppers, through the police, and on this occasion we have been in discussion with the bank in respect of it and the bank have chosen at this stage not to post a reward. In my experience in these cases large rewards like that are never claimed but we can assure anybody who has any information that it will be treated confidentially, sensitively and their interest will be protected.

So I asked the bank for their thoughts on offering a reward. Colin Dundas explained their thinking:

> I think that's something that we take advice from the PSNI on. We have had discussions with them about that and at this point in time the advice and the decision is not to offer a reward. If their view was different, I think the bank would take a different view but we do have to take advice from those people who have more expertise in these situations than ourselves.

What did the police think of that response? Det. Supt Sproule again: 'We have had some discussions with the bank in respect of rewards. I wouldn't want to go into the detail of it.'

This apparent ambiguity over who was responsible for deciding whether or not there would be a reward was also something that came up when I explored the value of the bank's own CCTV footage.

In the plethora of material that was released by police in the days after the robbery, it was very noticeable that any footage of the unusual white Ford Transit van, with its rather rare tailgate, came from police cameras around the city centre area and beyond. The police found images of the van on their own CCTV footage around Belfast and at Sprucefield roundabout near Hillsborough, heading south towards Newry.

But no pictures from the bank's own CCTV cameras focused on the bullion bay entrance have been issued by police—which raises a serious question: Did the bank security cameras work on the day of the robbery?

Bank spokesman Colin Dundas was evasive when I asked him that question:

> Again, that is detail that at this stage is still subject to police investigation and our own internal review, so I don't want to get into that. It's not appropriate for me to get into fine details about security procedures on that day or generally.

I then put the same question to the man heading the inquiry at the time, Det. Supt Sproule: Did the bank's cameras yield any pictures of the robbers and the white van outside the bank? But the answer I got was non-committal, to say the least:

> We have seized CCTV from throughout central Belfast but also much wider round west Belfast where we believe vehicles may have been, but also between Newry and Belfast . . . we know the van was seen south of Newry at ten to five on the evening of the robbery. So we know that there was a connection between Belfast and Newry, and just yesterday we discovered CCTV footage which appeared to show the van travelling south after the robbery at Sprucefield roundabout.

But were there any pictures? Neither the bank nor the police answered the question . . . so I took *those* evasive answers to mean no—that there were few pictures of any value from the bank's cameras.

I was told the problem with the bank's own footage was that the videotapes had been used and re-used so often by the bank's security cameras that the picture quality was badly degraded—with the images barely visible. But I was also told that had the images been of acceptable quality, they would have been publicised by the investigating officers.

It is quite startling to think that the bank's CCTV equipment, which is, after all, on the front line of defences against theft and robbery, should prove to be totally inadequate at its most important time of need.

The bank did successfully film one aspect of the robbery . . . the disappearing million pounds. Police released pictures of Chris Ward leaving the bank carrying a sports bag over his shoulder. These images were taken by the bank's CCTV camera positioned inside the staff entrance to the bank, located behind the security control room, which is facing the other direction into the bullion bay.

Those in charge of the bank security review studied these pictures. They seem to highlight another serious breach. Ward is disappearing from inside the cash centre with £1m in his sports bag, but why, oh why, was he not searched?

I asked Colin Dundas to explain: 'Well, I think it still comes back to the fact that the individual was under very specific instructions and under duress.'

> *AUTHOR*: I know he was, but did security not pick him up?
> *DUNDAS*: The entrance and exit for all staff coming in and out of the building was the entrance and exit which was used in that case, so it's not unusual to see people coming in or out of the building through that entrance.
> *AUTHOR*: But what about the sports bag over his shoulder? Are they searched as they come and go?
> *DUNDAS*: Without getting into the very specifics of it, again it would not be in itself unusual for a member of staff to bring sports gear in and out of the bank on a daily basis and go to the gym at lunchtime. What I'm saying is that a sports bag over someone's shoulder as a member of staff coming in and out is not unusual, but in terms of getting into the detail of what happened in this event, no, I think that's part of the overall review.

What is staggering about this £1m drop to the robbers is that staff could come and go from the cash centre carrying sports bags over their shoulders. Shouldn't they have had a locker room *outside* the cash centre? That way everyone entering and leaving the cash centre would have no visible means of taking some of the loot with them. And surely the bank must have been aware of the high-profile case a few years earlier involving the Ulster Bank where three low-paid messengers in their cash centre at Waring Street managed to take over £1m in used notes that were destined for the incinerator.

In the case of the Ulster Bank, its executives had to be alerted by another banking institution to the fact that one of their messengers had been salting away large sums of cash into a savings account. When confronted with the facts, it seems the bank did not believe it was possible to steal untraceable, used notes that were placed in the bank's own incinerator for destruction.

Even more staggering is that the Ulster Bank had no CCTV cameras in the cash centre where the money is sorted and counted, nor did they have a camera in the 'burn room'. But once police put a camera inside, they caught three Ulster Bank staff stealing the old notes out of the incinerator before it fired up . . . and this in spite of the fact that management loaded the counted notes into the burner and locked the incinerator, apparently making it impossible for anyone to steal any of the cash. Wrong!

The messengers had worked out how to bypass this security arrangement. There were two padlocks on the door of the incinerator. The keys for one lock were held by the messengers; the keys for the other by management. On the day of a 'burn', the messengers would open their lock and the management theirs early in the day. This was to permit the messengers to clean and prepare the burner for that day's delivery of old notes.

Once the money was loaded, the messengers would put their lock on the door and the management would do likewise. The management would then check that both locks had been shut and secured properly. The burner would be switched on. At this point they left the burn room to return to their duties. They believed their system was foolproof.

It took the burner ten minutes to heat up and ignite. And the messengers, meanwhile, had figured out a way of getting to the old notes inside the burner before the ignition. They bought a lock for around a fiver in a local hardware shop.

When the doors were opened in the morning for cleaning and preparation, they simply replaced the bank's open padlock with the padlock they had purchased themselves. They stashed the bank's padlock in a safe place until the machine was loaded. When they handed the bank executives their padlock to secure the door after loading, it was actually their own padlock. The bank messengers now had keys for the two padlocks and could open the burner to remove the cash—taking care to put the bank padlock on when they finished, keeping the one they bought safe for next time.

Naturally, bank officials had their complacency and confidence shattered when they found they had been so easily hoodwinked.

Now obviously that robbery had no bearing on the situation at the Northern Bank. But it is important because it illustrates very clearly that bank security is vulnerable—even internally, never mind the threat from outside individuals and organisations. The Ulster Bank experience should have been taken to heart by all banking institutions. But it wasn't.

John Horan worked on the Ulster Bank case and he feels the lessons to be learned went unheeded:

> I don't think the banks have learned anything. I think the classic example is the Ulster Bank where the messengers, who were absolutely poorly paid, had access to millions of pounds of money in an area where it was treated like confetti, and so, because it was treated like confetti, I believe they took it for that reason—because there was no value given to it and the bank did not put a high enough security team in to watch it.

The most important lesson to emerge from the Ulster Bank situation was that the bank should have had security in the cash centre, the vaults and the burn room.

In short, the Northern Bank should have had cameras in the cash centre vault that would have—on the night of the robbery —allowed security staff to see what was going on in the cash centre. They could have watched Ward and McMullan load the 'rubbish' on to trolleys! They could have seen the brand new 'rubbish' being removed, still in its wrapping from the printers!

The Ulster Bank lesson had not been learned, and now the bank was left scrambling around trying to ask itself why and how this had happened and why they had so little evidence to provide to the police.

Today, after the loss of £26m, there are cameras in the cash centre and in the vault. And the whole CCTV system has been overhauled. If a white van arrives to collect rubbish now, the security control room will have every angle covered with the latest digital security equipment. No more worn-out tapes in almost obsolete equipment.

As Richard told me:

> The equipment in the control room at the time of the robbery had been state of the art when it was originally installed. But no money was spent on upgrading, and it left security staff with small 4-inch monitors to look at. The quality of the equipment was awful. That's all been updated now and the bank has once again got state of the art equipment. There are now more and bigger screens showing what's going on in the cash centre and in the vault. The bank quickly accepted that the systems were not adequate.

This lack of investment in what is perhaps the most important aspect of banking—security—is typical of the way the Australian owners regarded their responsibilities, according to bank staff. As we will learn later, the Aussie owners had their own difficulties at home and needed to take as much cash out of the bank as they could lay their hands on.

There were two other significant changes made in the aftermath of the robbery. Richard explained those to me:

> After the robbery a cloakroom has been provided outside the sanitised area of the cash centre and that means that no one will ever again be able to take a sports bag into the cash centre

area. Now staff use the cloakroom to leave their jackets and sports bags or shopping bags outside before going into the cash centre.

And the other change has come at those internal security doors. Now we have a security man permanently on duty there. His job is to control those doors while staff are in the cash centre. It was felt this would be a good move, given that the supervisors in the centre no longer have the over-riding facility with the keys.

The replacement of security equipment and changes to the security regime are no doubt expensive. But the bank seems to accept that these changes are necessary.

The initial 'knee-jerk' reaction to the robbery meant that security staff carried the brunt of the criticism. The Chief Executive of the bank determined that the three Maybins security staff who would not be permitted to remain in their posts would be the site security manager and two security staff who were in the control room on the night of the robbery.

Only one of the two men in the security control room that night was actually on duty . . . the second man, a pensioner who worked part-time for Maybins, was present because he was to get a lift home with the man who was on duty. It appears the bank took the view that the pensioner distracted his friend and work colleague from his duties.

What was most unhelpful for the security staff was the fact that a young couple pushing a baby in a small pram noticed what they thought was something suspicious about the men in the white van as they were walking past. They talked it over as they headed down Donegall Place in front of the City Hall and when they saw a traffic warden, they stopped him and reported their suspicions. What they told him was that the men in the white van parked at the side of the Northern Bank appeared to be wearing baseball caps and wigs.

Strangers on the street could spot this but yet the security staff at the bank failed to notice anything untoward about the men who had arrived to collect rubbish . . . but perhaps it was the poor quality of the CCTV pictures which helped the robbers get away.

In any event, the traffic warden contacted police, and officers were sent around to the bank . . . arriving a few minutes after the van left the area. The officers did not knock on the door of the bank to speak to security staff.

I asked Det. Supt Andy Sproule about that:

We have interviewed those individuals. They did confirm that they saw a van with two people wearing wigs and baseball caps in the area of Wellington Street at around eight o'clock. They walked to a traffic warden, reported to the traffic warden what they had seen and the traffic warden reported it, telephoned it to police.

Unfortunately the police officers who were dispatched to the scene got the call at one minute after we know from CCTV that the van had left the street but there was no evidence of a crime scene when they were there and indeed, had the police officers rung the bank or any of the other business premises there, they wouldn't have known that anything untoward had occurred.

AUTHOR: Did they rap the door of the bank when they made their way round to it?
SPROULE: No, because there was no indication from the couple that the van was in any way connected to the bank. The couple did not connect the bank and a possible robbery to that van.
AUTHOR: All they saw was something that alerted them or raised suspicions with them?
SPROULE: Yes.
AUTHOR: And that was wigs and baseball caps?
SPROULE: Yes, what looked like wigs and one individual with a wig and a baseball cap.

Of course, hindsight is a wonderful thing. But is it not fair to ask the question of police: Do you depend on members of the public, untrained in the ways of criminals, to make the connection between men in baseball caps and wigs acting suspiciously outside a bank and a potential robbery? Is that not something that the police officers involved should have been a little more diligent about?

It's easy to say that even if they had knocked on the door of the bank, no one inside would have been aware that there had been a robbery. But, equally, had the officers knocked on the door of the bank and spoken to security staff inside to tell them that a member of the public had reported seeing men in baseball caps and wigs hanging around a white van parked outside and acting suspiciously, then it might have raised some alarm bells with the bank security staff. For a start, they might have been concerned about the wigs on men who had been at the bank in a white van a short time earlier. The poor quality of the CCTV images would have prevented them from noticing wigs on the men who called to collect rubbish. And that information could have sparked other trains of thought.

It might just have made the security staff think about everything else that night that was not normal routine . . . the white van remaining out in the street . . . twice by this stage . . . collecting rubbish after normal business hours. It might just have raised some concerns.

And guess what? Had those concerns been raised just after the white van had made its second run of the night, then the people to talk to were right there, in the bank, in the cash centre . . . Kevin McMullan and Chris Ward. Who knows what they might have felt obliged to tell police at that stage.

A bit more diligence from the police might have raised the alarm about a robbery minutes after the van had left the building . . . and might have given them an opportunity to meet the gang of criminals as they left Ward's house in Poleglass.

That is something we will never know. But I fancy the police authorities in their heart of hearts know that an opportunity was missed. This was a report that was not fully followed up.

The police are there to help stop and detect crimes. Of course they need co-operation from helpful members of the public . . . but it is not acceptable to expect the public to make the connection between incidents of suspicious activity and criminal activity.

According to one of my bank sources, it was around this time —just a few weeks after the robbery—that there developed a tension between the bank and the police.

As my source explained:

> After the robbery, the bank was told by the cops not to go public with anything . . . that they, the police, would deal with all media communications. But eventually the bank realised that the police were merely taking the initiative to avoid revealing their own shortcomings—such as the way they reacted to the report from the young couple, with baby in pram, who saw suspicious activity of men in wigs at the bank during the robbery.
>
> The bank resented the way the police were dealing with publicity. They did not like the way they were being told to 'shut up' by the police. There was also the issue of a failure from the police side to get any hint of such a robbery and this was considered in the aftermath of a difficult period three years ago when there was a real spate of such kidnappings and attacks on banks. The police at the time seemed to be suffering from the change-over from RUC to PSNI with the loss of many experienced officers.

According to my source, things were so bad that the security firm Securicor threatened to pull out of Northern Ireland. The whole situation was 'out of control'. My source recalled that at the time the then Security Minister Angela Smith caused upset in banking circles when she said something along the lines of having other priorities.

So if the security staff at the bank and the police have some questions to answer about their failings that night, the question must also be asked of management at the bank. What were their failings that created the circumstances when so many factors went against them and subsequently impacted on the chances of detecting those involved?

The ultimate responsibility for failing security equipment is down to the men who, in saving money by not regularly upgrading security equipment, actually stand accused of downgrading security—the management.

As John Horan put it:

> The bottom line is that the Chief Executives who make the decisions in these cases, they make it on the basis of commercialism. Is this going to happen to us again? No, probably not. That's their thought pattern, but the reality of it is there are people out there who are planning every day to rob and steal. They've nothing else to do, so I don't think any lessons have been learned. Lessons are only learned when something goes wrong with the security department in the bank, but of course they have to be ratified by higher up the chain and because it's going to cost money it doesn't get ratified.

If the management had become complacent in their attitude to security, then security staff faced the same kind of complacency in their daily work routine. That 'routine', of itself, is an enemy to good security, as John Horan explained:

> Security by its nature, the job itself, is repetitive and boring. You're not expecting that to happen. It was a good time to strike, coming up to Christmas. The security officers would have been preoccupied with their own personal lives and preoccupied with what they were going to do over Christmas and bored I would imagine. Now, of course, they will be in a very, very high state of alert, but give it a year and they will go back to the same line.

So on the day, the biggest weakness in the entire security system was the human element. Aside from the obvious human duress applied to the two staff from the cash centre, there's the whole debacle of how the bank's security staff performed.

It's a pattern seen so many times before by Jonty Brown:

It is a failing, absolutely. Of course it's a failing but you're talking again about human element. They knew, the security officers in the control room and on the ground would have known those two members of staff, so with that your guard is down. If you've got chairs sticking out of the bags and you've got wastepaper, you've got rubbish and you're told by two staff employees that it's rubbish, well, it's human nature to immediately assume 'yes it's rubbish' and allow them to proceed.

AUTHOR: That's their weakness?

BROWN: Yes, of course it is, but again they used the human element, the weakest link, to get it past the security guards. The security guard, can you castigate him? I don't believe you can, because he's told they're coming out with rubbish.

John Horan agrees:

By their nature security guards are supposed to be distrustful of everyone, including the insider, but human nature means that when they work in an environment they start to trust and know and like the people they work with and you never think ill of one until something like this happens.

AUTHOR: Now we're told that there was a security presence in the control room and that this money was coming down past them. Does that surprise you?

HORAN: No. You're back to the human factor. You're making the assumption, or sorry the assumption is being made that the security guard on duty was giving it 100% attention, that he was focused on what he was doing. He may not have been in the control room. He may have taken a comfort break. He may have been watching a different monitor. He may just have been day-dreaming and not doing his job. I don't know, not being there, but again bringing the human factor into it, this is what this gentleman does day in day out and I would imagine he was very bored.

There was nothing boring about the bank's security review, however, which began with a meeting two days after the robbery with the Chief Executive. The main concern was that this was an inside job.

It was very quickly apparent to the kidnapped bank staff that the gang already knew the bank inside out. They knew by the nature of the questions they were being asked . . . and by the gang's knowledge of their personal details. Then there was the fact that the robbers had even been able to identify the pair as the key-holders of the safe on this particular date . . . even though the rota that put them together had only been finalised forty-eight hours earlier on the Friday and had been changed at the last moment. Conclusion? This was an inside job. And that was the conclusion of the Northern Bank management at their security review.

Jonty Brown told me it was a cut and dried case:

> Whoever gave them the inside information I would say they were milked dry. Every aspect of security that could be breached was examined, re-examined. They would have sat and thought about how else could the Northern Bank get round this to make sure there was no other way.

This is still an issue to be resolved by the police and the bank. As far as the bank is concerned, there is still an IRA 'mole' on the inside . . . someone who had engaged in an act of betrayal.

Aside from providing the gang with details about staffing arrangements in the cash centre, information about how internal security operates and vital detail about security codes and key-holders, the 'insider' may well have provided the gang with the bank's published security arrangements in the event of a kidnapping.

At least in making their analysis after the event, bank executives would have to consider the possibility—however unpalatable—that whoever was working with the gang inside the bank would have been persuaded to hand over all information that was likely to be of use to the gang . . . including the bank's security briefing to staff on kidnappings.

This document, reproduced below, would help the robbers plan their operation—making them aware of how staff are supposed to respond in the event of a kidnapping and how they are supposed to detect one in advance.

I have concealed the special telephone numbers provided by the bank for staff to raise the alarm—but it is almost certain the gang of kidnapping robbers would have had access to this document. This is what bank staff are told about kidnappings and how to avoid them:

KIDNAPPINGS: A GUIDE TO PREVENTION—DECEMBER 2004

General

The very fact that we work in the Banking Industry makes us prone to kidnapping. Fortunately the risk is low and with some insight into how they happen the risk can be reduced further. The objective of kidnappers [is to] get what they want, usually money, and make their escape before they are caught by the authorities.

In this booklet the risks of kidnapping are outlined, together with how a kidnapper goes about identifying an individual for kidnapping. Preventative measures are also discussed along with what to do in the unlikely event that a kidnapping occurs.

Why Do Kidnappings Happen?
There are generally 3 reasons why kidnappings happen:
for cash
for political reasons
for publicity
Cash is usually the primary motivating factor in a kidnapping. This can either be hard cash or some form of electronic transfer of funds.
Political kidnappings do occur from time to time although they usually happen in such areas as the Middle East or Africa.
Kidnappings for publicity are rare but will happen if a group

wants to draw attention to their particular cause.

The Risk
The risk of kidnapping is posed mainly by 2 distinct groups:
Criminals and Terrorists
Crack Pots
Kidnappers may be motivated for different reasons. The ransom money is either for personal gain or for funding an organisation, however the effect is the same. Determined criminals and terrorists have the expertise, the skills and the resolution to attempt a kidnapping.
If a kidnapping does happen it will be completely out of the blue, life will be going on as normal when the following will happen:
Extremely aggressive armed men will probably force their way into your house.
They will push, shove, shout and will tie up you and your family. They may take you and your family away to another building, where they will feel safe and from where they cannot be traced.
They will issue threats and will demand that you do as you are told. They want to get the ransom money and escape.
However, it doesn't have to be that way. Kidnappers do not just stroll past your house one day and decide to kidnap you and your family. They will plan the operation. They will prepare by:
Selecting the individual who can give them what they want.
Once selected they will gain information about that individual, where they live, what routes they take to work and how their home is laid out.
This type of information takes months to accumulate. It will involve the kidnappers following your car, visiting your home and making telephone calls to your work. It is during this preparatory phase that they can give themselves away.

THE GIVE AWAY CLUES

At Home
If the kidnapping is to take place at home the kidnappers have to establish what your home is like. They need to know its general

layout, where you and your family spend your evenings, are there any dogs in the house, do you have an alarm system etc? The list is long and they have methods in which they gather that information. Some of the methods are:

Unexpected visitors will come to the house and will try to gain entry by bluffing their way in. It may be people trying to sell you something or others claiming to be from the electricity or telephone company.

The telephone will be used to contact your home to confirm that you are who they think you are. The phone book will be used to establish your address. Children are very easy to get information out of and will answer questions truthfully, such as, "Does your dad work in the bank?"

All of us have probably lived in the same house for some years and so have known neighbours. Over time patterns are established and we notice things such as the person opposite always cleans their car on a Sunday morning. What is being looked for are people who change that standard pattern, perhaps it is a person jogging or it may be someone pushing a pram.

Travel
Do not just assume that the kidnappers are only interested in your travel to and from work. It may be that they are interested in establishing where and what your leisure activities are. To find out how you travel they may have to follow you.

If you are using a car they will attempt to follow it, but the methods they use are not those seen in films. They will not be driving at breakneck speed, two feet from your bumper. They will be following 2 or 3 vehicles behind using the vehicles as cover. In addition they may be in front of you and again they may use 2 or 3 vehicles as cover. If you think that another vehicle is watching/following you, take a circular route back onto your original road. By doing this you may be able to establish if you are being followed.

At Work
At work all employees should be aware of the kidnapping threat

and be aware of strangers asking questions that are out of the ordinary. This would include:
Where do you live?
What clubs do you belong to?
Where do the children go to school?

The Solution
The kidnappers have to gain information, they need to know as much about you as possible. It is during this planning phase that they can give themselves away. By doing things yourself you can reduce the risk:

REDUCE THE RISK BY:
Noting anything unusual, this includes people and vehicles. Get descriptions of both (see Descriptions Section later).
Reporting what you see to Security Services.
Be vigilant and be seen to be taking notice of what is going on. When you come out of your house look around and see what is happening, are there any strange vehicles parked? Let people see that you are observant. Ask strangers if you can help them, let them know that you see them. This type of action indicates to any potential kidnapper that you are aware of what is going on and it may be enough to deter them from carrying out a kidnapping in the first place.

What To Do If a Kidnapping Happens
If a kidnapping does happen there are 3 things you should do:
Stay calm. Although the situation is very frightening it is important to stay calm. The kidnappers themselves will be anxious and it is best not to increase their anxiety as they may hit out.
Obey. Do what the kidnappers tell you to do, there is no point in annoying them.
Report the incident at the earliest opportunity to **** *** *** from Northern Ireland or * *** *** *** from the Republic of Ireland.—See Actions to be taken.

Actions To Be Taken

It is important that you should do the following, this will ensure that the kidnapping is resolved successfully. For everyone and that includes yourself, the bank and the police, the successful conclusion of a kidnapping is the safe return of the kidnapped victim.

Listen to what the kidnappers are telling you and make sure you understand it.

Verify what they want—how do they want the money made up—how and where do they want it delivered.

At the earliest opportunity telephone the 24 hour Help Line. This will be answered and help will be at hand. The telephone number is:

From Northern Ireland—**** *** ***

From Republic of Ireland—* *** *** ***

It is important that the kidnappers are stalled so that there is enough time to respond to what they want. This isn't difficult, simply tell them the truth i.e. the cash is under time lock, there is dual control and it takes time to make up money.

Do Not

There are three things which you should not do:

Do not telephone the local police. This is a police requirement. They need to be able to respond in the correct way and do not want the local car with sirens wailing and lights flashing chasing down the road.

Do not pay out. While this may seem strange and it may be tempting to do so, it can be dangerous. Firstly a kidnap may not have occurred. Secondly, if they get away with it once, the kidnappers may come back again. Thirdly, the victim may not be returned.

Do not talk to the press. Refer any enquiries to Corporate Relations at *** ******** from Northern Ireland or *** **** **** from the Republic of Ireland.

Descriptions

It is important that descriptions are remembered which enable *the police to carry out their investigations. The methods used are simple and in the case of people should be approximations.*

People—The Alphabet Method

A—Age
B—Build
C—Colour
D—Distinguishing Marks
E—Elevation (height)
F—Facial features
G—Gait, how do they walk
H—Hair, colour, how much of it.

Vehicles

S—Shape—hatchback, saloon
C—Colour
R—Registration
I—Identification
M—Make

Summary

Kidnappings are an ever-present risk in the banking industry, however the risk is low and with the measures described above can be further reduced. Kidnappings do take planning and it is during the planning phase when the kidnappers can either give themselves away or can be put off.

It is important to co-operate with the kidnappers to avoid putting either yourself or your family's well-being at risk. While you should do what they tell you, remember to report the incident as soon as possible and play for time. The longer the kidnappers have to wait, the more chance there is of them going away not only empty handed but more importantly leaving your family safe. You should not however be tempted to pay out, it is not the answer and may only result in further trouble.

If you have any concerns over kidnapping or wish to report any suspicious incidents please contact Security Services at *** **** **** from Northern Ireland or *** **** **** from Republic of Ireland.

Consider the information in this document. In many ways, it describes exactly what happened to two members of the Northern Bank's staff. Remember Chris Ward's thoughts as he was questioned and taken away by members of the gang. He was amazed about the amount of knowledge the kidnappers had of his family and his leisure time as an office-bearer in a Celtic Football Supporters Club, and he began to have thoughts about how members of the gang must have followed him around to help them work out these personal details of his life.

But if the gang had someone on the inside, a lot of the pain of following staff and trying to work out their daily routine would have been removed. All the precautions in the world cannot compete with someone who is prepared to betray colleagues and employers.

So, at that first management meeting two days after the embarrassing £26m robbery, the Northern Bank would have to consider, carefully, how it responded to the security issues following the raid, given that the police and bank security staff had already determined that the robbers had a mole on the inside. Even more disturbing was the thought that that person was still working in the bank, going about their daily business as usual.

If the priority was to devise a security system that would frustrate any future attack, the bank would have to implement whatever measures were considered necessary but with the certain knowledge that someone within the bank was in a position to pass that vital new information on to any would-be raiders for future reference.

Some of the new measures would have to be established in a way that would take account of the likelihood that there was a mole working inside the bank—someone who had already passed on crucial security information to aid the robbers to get away with millions.

For a start, the police made it clear that everyone working in the cash centre would have to be considered suspect until the investigation was in a position to clear those forty or so individuals as the inquiry progressed. The bank had already decided to re-deploy everyone who worked in the cash centre.

The police had concentrated their efforts from the outset on trying to unmask the 'insider' working with the gang of robbers. Det. Supt Sproule told me:

> We said at a very early stage that that was one of the lines of enquiry that we were conducting. The terrorists who were involved in this operation knew some of the inner workings of the bank. Now how they acquired that knowledge we still don't know. It is a very important line of enquiry. It was important to have two key-holders in position, whether it was those two [Ward and McMullan] or any number of the other key-holders. On that particular night these two unfortunate individuals and their families were subject to a horrific ordeal and the individuals certainly are not the better of it now and they may never be.

Nevertheless, as Jonty Brown explained, the police must start their investigation at the source of the call alerting them to the problem. That meant looking closely at Chris Ward and Kevin McMullan.

The publicity following the robbery left Chris Ward feeling angry and upset. He felt it was unfair to isolate him as a young Catholic from west Belfast and do as the press did, bring into question his involvement with a Celtic supporters' club as a means of starting a 'whispering campaign'.

He said it concerned him greatly that elements of the media put out what he described as 'ludicrous reports and stories' relating to him and his personal life. He was particularly upset about references to where he drank and the football club he supported, and he felt this was being done because of his religion and because of the area he lived in.

In spite of the clearly stated instructions in the bank's kidnap procedures document that staff should not speak to the media directly, but rather refer them to the bank's publicity department, Chris Ward decided to go public to refute the insinuations about him in the media.

He told reporters it was absolutely horrendous to think that because he was a Catholic from west Belfast, people were perceiving that he was in some way involved in the robbery. He said he and his family were trying to recover from one of the most horrible, hurtful and terrible ordeals that anyone's had to go through. And while trying to deal with all of that he picks up newspapers and reads stories about his personal life—about where he drinks and the football club he supports.

He told the *Irish News*:

There have been stories saying that I am a Celtic supporter and I am from west Belfast. They don't say it directly but there is an insinuation that because I am a west Belfast Catholic that I must have been part of the robbery.

My family has been deeply traumatised by what we were put through. Those stories have just made things worse. Would anyone put their loved ones through such an ordeal? I know I certainly wouldn't and neither would Kevin McMullan.

Ward also recorded an interview with the BBC's *Spotlight* programme. When reporter Kevin Magee asked him how his family was coping, he replied:

It's a very, very difficult time for them. It's been four weeks today, today's Monday isn't it, four weeks it is now. This time four weeks ago was right in the heart of what was happening and still from that time four weeks ago my mum and my dad, worse for my mum and my dad, are very traumatised with it, my brother as well but he's a young man too and he's stronger than my mum and dad, you know. They're very traumatised from it. It's a very terrible experience. You know when people call to the door they're very nervy about going to the door, you know, and it's really up to us as a family to try and be strong and stick together and try and get through this terrible ordeal, but hopefully we will . . . but it's very, very hard for them, and of course then when they read media about me, because my mum made a comment to one of the police persons, she says 'he's only a young man, he's from Poleglass in west Belfast. What are people going to think, you know' because at that stage she didn't know that there was both Kevin and I involved, you know, until Kevin came to the house that night, so you know it's very, very hard for them. They're going through a very terrible time, you know.

Maybe it was Chris Ward himself who was badly traumatised, but his reference to his mum's comments to the police did not make sense given everything else he had told the BBC and the *Irish News*. If his previous comments were correct, then by the time his mother was speaking to anyone from the police it must have been after Ward and McMullan left work following the robbery and travelled to Ward's home in Poleglass.

Members of the kidnap gang were still present and it was only twenty minutes after they left that McMullan departed for his home in Loughinisland. So he met Ward's family before contact was made with police. That only happened some time after McMullan left the Ward home when Ward, as instructed by his kidnappers, reported the robbery to police at 11 p.m.

After the trauma of being kidnapped and knowing that his family was at risk of death if he did not comply with the wishes of the gang of robbers, perhaps Chris Ward was simply confused about what his mum said to police and when she said it.

I spoke to Chris Ward on a number of occasions in an attempt to persuade him to do an interview for a one-hour film I was preparing for UTV's *Insight* programme. He explained that he didn't want to go beyond what he had said to the *Irish News* and the BBC. I sought clarification from him on the point he made about his mother speaking to police; about how he had said that was before she had known Kevin McMullan was involved as well and about how McMullan had met his mother some time before the police arrived. This is what he said:

Oh aye, aye, but if you heard what I said that was before, let me think what I'm trying to say to you. You see I don't really

want to comment on it and honest to God, Chris, I just don't
want to be making any comment so that in a couple of weeks
time you think . . .

AUTHOR: No, but do you understand what I'm saying.

WARD: I understand what you're saying.

AUTHOR: If your mum was talking to the policeman, it had
to be after you had made the call to the police and that would
have been after she had met Kevin because you came to your
house after the whole thing was over?

WARD: Honest to God, Chris, I know the answer in my head
but I don't want to go into it. I'm being honest now, I would
ask you that you appreciate this—that I don't want to make
any further comment.

AUTHOR: But if you would only clarify that for me?

WARD: I don't feel there's the necessity to. I mean I've went
out. We made the two media through the *Irish News* and the
BBC and as far as I'm concerned I don't want to speak about it
ever again and that's . . . I was speaking to my solicitor this
morning and he says, 'Look if you want to, it's up to you'. His
advice obviously is, you know, 'it's up to you if you want to go
to the media', but he was advising as a solicitor not to and
what I've said I've said and I'm going to stick with that. Chris,
please appreciate that mate, and I don't want to talk about
anything that happened to be honest with you. I just want it
left. I know you're probably complaining and I know I'm
messing you. I mean you have a job to do but again my
apologies about the programme. Obviously you wanted me
involved. I don't want to be involved. As far as I want to be is
just put this to bed and move on with my life. Alright mate.

There's no doubt Chris Ward endured a horrendous ordeal.
Whether life will ever be the same again for the young west
Belfast man is unclear. Similarly, Kevin and Karen McMullan will
have great difficulty getting back to normal.

But while Chris Ward and Kevin McMullan struggle with their
own feelings, they will have been aware that for a time at least

they would have to be considered as suspects in the robbery as the police began the task of hunting down the gang responsible.

In the months after the raid they, like many others employed in the Northern Bank's headquarters, would have been placed under police surveillance, not to mention closer scrutiny by the bank itself.

Police surveillance revealed that Chris Ward took a holiday to Lanzarote. What surprised police was that his girlfriend, with whom he had split up in the weeks preceding the robbery, also travelled to Lanzarote on the same day, on the same plane.

She is also a Northern Bank employee, although at a different branch. And what also for a time intrigued police is the fact that her father is a well-known republican.

In effect, Chris Ward has probably felt himself to be in a strange position—along of course with Kevin McMullan. Both men were victims of armed raiders and yet for a time at least they were—along with everyone else that worked in the cash centre—considered suspects.

In the weeks immediately after the robbery, life was extremely difficult for Chris Ward, his parents and family, and for Karen and Kevin McMullan. One bank source told me that the McMullans were very traumatised.

Karen McMullan was so mentally upset that it showed visibly. She found it difficult to focus her attention and was always very close to tears, while husband Kevin often physically shook, his hands at times appearing to behave as if out of control. He was constantly looking over his shoulder because of the now permanent feeling that someone was watching and following him.

Chris Ward was also heavily traumatised. He perhaps found some relief through his love of Celtic Football Club. At least going to the games he could momentarily forget what had happened and hide among the 60,000 other fans attending games at Parkhead in Glasgow.

But there is no doubt that the dramatic and terrifying events of Christmas 2004 will remain with the Ward and McMullan families for years to come.

It was some considerable time before the two bank staff could return to work. They were under no pressure from the bank. They were told to take all the time necessary to overcome the trauma of the events of 19 and 20 December. By October 2005, the two men were ready to return to work.

But things at work may never be the same again for either of them. I understand that initially, Kevin McMullan was placed in the bank's department responsible for ATMs. His return to work was not announced in advance, although some staff felt that the bank should have let people know he was coming back to work.

After the initial adverse reaction of staff in the cash centre who were transferred to other duties following the robbery, there's now an understanding as to why it was so essential.

One staff member explained:

> We were resentful at first, but now I think we can understand the reasoning behind the bank's decision. I don't think the bank had any alternative. Many were three-quarters way through their careers and felt dirty because the shadow of suspicion was being placed over them all by the attitude of management.
>
> The management angle was that we were being moved for our own good. Management accepted there was a mole and that the mole could have passed on every detail of all nine members of staff who were key-holders. As management said at the time, we had to be moved in case our details were already in the hands of terrorists and we might in the future become targets.

The McMullans and Chris Ward have received counselling provided by the bank. Chris Ward acknowledged the bank's assistance during his media interviews, telling the BBC:

> The bank have been very supportive, yeah. They've been very supportive and we went to a counselling session as a family about a week and a half ago and we follow that up then with individual counselling sessions provided by the bank, so yeah, it's been very supportive of them.

By now the police will have examined a great deal of information and made determinations that simply could not be made in the early days of their investigation, and they alone know how much progress has been made towards arresting the gang responsible and bringing them before the courts.

Looking back at the events that led to the robbery, both the police and the bank will have consulted about how security failed, and how to take steps to make sure it cannot happen again. Both will continue their search for the mole inside who conspired with the raiders . . . and who still poses a risk to future security and indeed to the investigation itself.

And while the police ponder what might have happened if the officers who arrived at the bank moments after the white van left had knocked on the door of the bank, the bank will reflect that the changes in the control of the keys used by supervisors was a day too late to deter the robbers.

As Chris Ward and Kevin McMullan left the bank on Monday 20 December 2004, McMullan handed in their keys to the security man at the door.

Things would never be the same again for them, or for the bank.

05 ANNUS HORRIBILIS

'The Provos did it,' cried the unionists.

'Oh no they didn't,' cried the Provos.

'Oh yes they did,' cried the Chief Constable.

'Oh no they didn't,' cried Sinn Féin.

'Oh yes they did,' cried the British and Irish governments.

—

A ppropriately, it was pantomime season as the political blame game began over who was responsible for carrying out the Northern Bank robbery.

When news of the grand theft of £26m from the Northern Bank's Belfast headquarters broke, it was open season—not only on who was to blame for the robbery but on the whole peace process and the small matter of trusting partnerships in government.

The robbery had journalists and politicians immediately reaching for the latest report from the Independent Monitoring Commission (IMC), published a few weeks earlier in November. The Commission had noted that there were no signs that the IRA was winding down its capability. And it went on to cite the IRA's involvement in the theft of £1m worth of goods some months previously to illustrate this point.

The IMC quoted figures supplied by the Northern Ireland Organised Crime Task Force, which had reported that of the 230

organised criminal gangs in Northern Ireland, 140 of them—
that's 60 per cent—had paramilitary links. The task force also
said that two-thirds of the top twenty-five gangs involved in
international activities were linked to the paramilitaries.

The IMC was in no doubt about the impact of this criminal
activity when it concluded:

> Seldom in the developed world has this high proportion of
> serious criminals been associated with groups originating in
> terrorism, with an organisational structure and discipline,
> and the experience of planning and conducting sophisticated
> clandestine operations, methods of handling money and with
> traditions of violence.

Some commentators were moved to speculate that the robbery
was a republican response to the failed negotiations to re-instate
devolved government.

It was even argued that the robbery was made possible by the
long-term aims of republicans to handicap the police. The
Sunday Independent's Jim Cusack wrote on 9 January 2005:

> The key to the biggest bank raid in European history lay not
> so much in the skills of the IRA unit which carried out the
> heist, but in the creation of an environment where
> intelligence-driven policing in Northern Ireland was
> diminished almost to the point of ineffectiveness.
>
> Ten years ago when the RUC Special Branch was at the
> height of its effectiveness, this robbery simply would not have
> taken place. The Special Branch had moles inside the IRA
> leadership in Belfast, Derry, Tyrone and even south Armagh.
> Those days are gone. 'Policing reform' has been Sinn Féin's
> catch cry through the so-called peace process alongside a
> campaign to expose so-called 'collusion' by the RUC Special
> Branch.
>
> The Sinn Féin-led campaign against this so-called
> collusion received masses of media exposure, creating a
> situation where intelligence gathering became synonymous in

many people's minds with complicity in loyalist murder and terrorism, but intelligence-driven undercover policing is the most effective tool any police force has in combating organised crime.

This situation was virtually achieved about five months ago, when a direction was apparently given that the PSNI could no longer use informants with criminal records. This effectively meant the IRA had carte blanche to set up the operation to carry out the biggest bank heist in history.

The other key element from the IRA point of view was to place moles inside the bank who could provide details of the security systems and advise on the right time to strike.

Cusack went on to write that the placing of moles was evident in a number of other IRA operations—citing as an example the St Patrick's Day 2000 break-in at the headquarters of the Special Branch at Castlereagh police station in Belfast.

Cusack talked to his sources in west Belfast and was told that the robbery was the work of a well-known IRA gang—made up of young men recruited in recent years and trained to very high standards to carry out robberies and hijackings to help fund the republican movement.

He identified the core of the IRA leadership as being made up mainly of ex-prisoners who survived jail in the seventies and eighties during the protests and the hunger strike and leading up to the mass escape in 1983. Cusack described these individuals as well educated and capable of not only organising major operations, but also dictating the direction of the Provisionals.

He added:

The background to their collective planning abilities lies in the 1983 Maze breakout when thirty-eight IRA members fled what was supposedly Europe's highest security jail. The plan involved two years of preparations, beginning with the segregation of republican and loyalist prisoners—one of the 'five demands' sought by the hunger strikers. This segregation allowed Provisionals to prepare away from suspicious loyalist eyes. The core group of planners behind the breakout carried out their long-range collective planning into projects constructed in and around the 'peace process'.

The Northern Bank robbery cast even more uncertainty on the peace process and drew the sharp focus of attention once again on the real intentions of Sinn Féin and the IRA.

Once the PSNI's Chief Constable Hugh Orde pronounced that the police believed the robbery to be the work of the IRA, the British and Irish governments were quick to seize the opportunity to question the motives of the republican movement.

At the same time, stories were being leaked to the media that in the weeks before the robbery, the IRA had been telling its members that it was on the verge of disbandment. Senior republicans had apparently travelled extensively in the Republic to inform the membership of the decision to throw everything into the power-sharing executive at Stormont.

Throughout it all, Sinn Féin maintained that the IRA had not been responsible for the robbery. At various times Martin McGuinness and Gerry Adams told reporters that they had spoken to the IRA and had been told that it was not involved. They said they believed the IRA when it said it was not involved.

But like it or not, Sinn Féin found themselves on the back foot trying to maintain confidence in their commitment to securing peace through IRA disarmament and political dialogue. It was a battle on three fronts—with the British government, their friends in America and with the government in Dublin.

To use the parlance of the times, Dublin became a 'cold house' for republicans. Taoiseach Bertie Ahern was not impressed by Sinn Féin's denials that republicans or members of the IRA were involved in the robbery. In fact, he made comments which angered Gerry Adams. No, they unfuriated Gerry Adams.

The trouble began when the Taoiseach agreed with Hugh Orde that it was the IRA who carried out the Northern Bank raid. Of course, the reason he really believed it was the Provos was because of the briefings he received from the Gardai and his own military intelligence service. The Taoiseach said Sinn Féin negotiators must have known about the robbery plans during talks on a political settlement in the weeks before the raid.

Gerry Adams demanded that the Taoiseach withdraw his allegations that he had prior knowledge of the Northern Bank raid or else have him charged with conspiracy to rob and withholding information. The Sinn Féin leader said:

> I think the Taoiseach has crossed the line. It's time for him to shut up or put up. I feel a particular sense of betrayal by the Taoiseach. I think the Taoiseach has crossed the line and the line that he has crossed—and I took legal advice on this—was to accuse Martin McGuinness and I of conspiracy to rob and of withholding information. I feel particularly angry about that.

Jim Cusack of the *Sunday Independent* told me:

> The view of the Gardaí is that it was the IRA, and they seem to think that there was a very senior member of the IRA from south Armagh who was either in charge of it or certainly involved in it in a fairly significant way. And they seemed to get that information quite quickly . . . and they seemed to be acting on their own from what I gather.
>
> The government's decision is based on security and intelligence reports here and that's from the Garda Síochána and also from the Defence Forces, the Irish Army's intelligence, their C3 Section, which acts independently from the Garda. They work together but I mean they basically have independent assessments in matters like this and both operate their own system of intelligence agents and sources and surveillance, so they apparently came up with virtually the same conclusion.
>
> And the Taoiseach's remarks about the Sinn Féin leadership being aware of this matter stems from the fact that one of the people who they were told was involved in this is a member of the Army Council, and the information going to

the Irish government from as I say the Army and the Gardai
would be that there are members of Sinn Féin leadership who
had dual membership of the IRA Army Council.

According to Cusack, the Irish government receives quarterly
intelligence reports on who is sitting on the IRA Army Council,
adding: 'That has always been the case and that still is the case,
and in the last report, from the latest reports, I gather that they
would say that yes, those two men are on the Army Council.'

But Bertie Ahern was not content to let matters rest there. In
the Dáil he was able to make the argument that the IRA had not
ceased all paramilitary activities in spite of the ceasefires. He had
a catalogue of crime which he said was the work of the IRA. He
ran off a long list of punishment shootings, beatings and
robberies going back a number of years.

Just as the IMC had done, the Taoiseach recalled the robberies
at Makro in Dunmurry when goods worth £1m were taken, the
abduction of people and theft of goods from an Iceland
supermarket in Strabane and the kidnapping of people and theft
of cigarettes worth £2m from a bonded delivery vehicle in Belfast.

There was just a whiff of hypocrisy to all this. If the IRA had
been responsible for these other crimes—and that was certainly
the belief of the police in Northern Ireland as well as the Gardaí
—then why did the governments in Dublin and London wait
until the £26m Northern Bank raid before mentioning them?
That was the question many people were asking as they watched
the continuing blame game unfold.

The accusations of criminality upset the IRA. They decided to
withdraw all co-operation with the decommissioning body. It
appeared to be a petulant response to the flak over the Northern
Bank robbery.

Here's how the IRA statement of 2 February 2005 announced
the change in arrangements:

In August 1994, the leadership of Óglaigh na hÉireann
announced a complete cessation of all military operations. We
did so to enhance the democratic peace process and underline

our definitive commitment to its success.

That cessation ended in February 1996 because the British Government acted in bad faith when the then British Prime Minister John Major and Unionist leaders squandered that unprecedented opportunity to resolve the conflict.

However, we remained ready to engage positively and in July 1997 we reinstated the cessation on the same basis as before. Subsequently, we honoured the terms of our cessation with discipline and honesty, despite numerous attempts to misrepresent those terms by others.

Since then—over a period of almost eight years—our leadership took a succession of significant and ambitious initiatives designed to develop or save the peace process. Those included:

Engaging with the Independent International Commission on Decommissioning;

Agreeing that independent inspectors could inspect the contents of a number of IRA dumps, allowing regular re-inspections to ensure that the weapons remained secure and the reporting of what they had done both publicly and to the IICD;

Setting out a clear context for dealing definitively with the issue of arms;

Acknowledging past mistakes, hurt and pain the IRA has caused to others and extending our sincere apologies and condolences for the deaths and injuries of non-combatants caused by us;

Agreeing a scheme with the IICD to put arms completely and verifiably beyond use;

Implementing this scheme to save the peace process by putting three separate tranches of weapons beyond use on:

– 23 October 2001
– 11 April 2002
– 21 October 2003; and

Seeking to directly and publicly address unionist concerns.

In 2004 our leadership was prepared to speedily resolve the issue of arms, by Christmas if possible, and to invite two independent witnesses, from the Protestant and Catholic churches, to testify to this. In the context of a comprehensive agreement we were also prepared to move into a new mode and to instruct our Volunteers that there could be no involvement whatsoever in activities which might endanger that agreement.

These significant and substantive initiatives were our contributions to the peace process. Others, however, did not share that agenda. Instead, they demanded the humiliation of the IRA.

Our initiatives have been attacked, devalued and dismissed by pro-unionist and anti-republican elements, including the British Government. The Irish Government have lent themselves to this. Commitments have been broken or withdrawn. The progress and change promised on political, social, economic and cultural matters, as well as on demilitarisation, prisoners, equality and policing and justice, has not materialised to the extent required, or promised.

British forces, including the PSNI, remain actively engaged in both covert and overt operations, including raids on republicans' homes. We are also acutely aware of the dangerous instability within militant unionism, much of it fostered by British military intelligence agencies. The British/loyalist apparatus for collusion remains intact. The political institutions have been suspended for years now and there is an ongoing political impasse.

At this time it appears that the two governments are intent on changing the basis of the peace process. They claim that "the obstacle now to a lasting and durable settlement is the continuing paramilitary and criminal activity of the IRA". We reject this. It also belies the fact that a possible agreement last December was squandered by both governments pandering to rejectionist unionism instead of upholding their own commitments and honouring their own obligations.

We do not intend to remain quiescent within this unacceptable and unstable situation. It has tried our patience to the limit. Consequently, on reassessment of our position and in response to the governments and others withdrawing their commitments;

We are taking all our proposals off the table.

It is our intention to closely monitor ongoing developments and to protect to the best of our ability the rights of republicans and our support base.

The IRA has demonstrated our commitment to the peace process again and again. We want it to succeed. We have played a key role in achieving the progress achieved so far. We are prepared, as part of a genuine and collective effort, to do so again, if and when the conditions are created for this.

But peace cannot be built on ultimatums, false and malicious accusations or bad faith. Progress will not be sustained by the reinstatment of Thatcherite criminalisation strategies, which our ten comrades died defeating on hunger strike in 1981. We will not betray the courage of the hunger strikers either by tolerating criminality within our own ranks or false allegations of criminality against our organisation by petty politicians motivated by selfish interests, instead of the national need for a successful conclusion to the peace process.

Finally, we thank all those who have supported us through decades of struggle. We freely acknowledge our responsibility to enhance genuine efforts to build peace and justice. We reiterate our commitment to achieving Irish independence and our other republican objectives. We are determined that these objectives will be secured.

The IRA was rejecting in the strongest possible terms the assertions that it had become a criminal organisation. This statement was issued just a few days after a death in Belfast that had not yet become linked to the Provisionals—but would soon bring world attention to the IRA. In the meantime, the republican movement was engaged in damage control as a result of a story published a month earlier about the Colombia Three. Things were going from bad to worse for republicans . . . 2005 was about to become an 'annus horribilis' for them.

On Sunday 19 December (the day before the robbery), the

front page of the *Sunday World*'s Northern edition told its readers that the three republicans convicted for seventeen years in their absence by a Colombian court three days earlier had sneaked into neighbouring Venezuela.

The paper reported that the three Irishmen arrested in Colombia in August 2001 using false travel documents—Martin McAuley from Lurgan in County Armagh; James Monaghan from County Donegal and Dubliner Niall Connolly—were either already in Cuba or still in Venezuela on their way to Cuba helped by a senior IRA man on the run.

Back in 2001, James Monaghan, a convicted bomb maker, Niall Connolly, reportedly Sinn Féin's unofficial representative for Latin America, and Martin McAuley, a suspected explosives expert with a conviction for possession of weapons, were put on public display by the Colombian authorities after their arrests.

The three startled-looking figures were filmed being escorted to a notorious Bogotá prison as the Colombians alleged they were an IRA engineering team on a training mission to Colombia. Their arrests came at a pivotal stage in the Colombian peace process that coincided with the decommissioning crisis in Ireland.

According to the *Sunday World*, Paul Damery, from Cork, masterminded the escape of the Colombian Three. Damery, the paper stated, was still wanted in the Republic for the murder of Garda detective Jerry McCabe.

Damery had moved to Venezuela to hide because his wife comes from the South American country, the paper reported.

McAuley, Monaghan and Connolly had gone on the run as well . . . initially in Colombia. They disappeared in June 2004 after being acquitted on charges of helping train left-wing FARC guerrillas in the Colombian jungle. FARC is shorthand for the Revolutionary Armed Forces of Colombia.

In April 2004—by which time devolved government had collapsed following a high-profile police search of Sinn Féin offices at Stormont, centred on what was described at the time as an IRA spy-ring at Parliament Buildings—the three Irishmen were found guilty of travelling on false passports but were cleared of training FARC terrorists.

After their acquittal, the prosecution appealed the case and a Bogotá court found them guilty and sentenced them to seventeen years imprisonment.

But by then they had fled the jurisdiction.

Warrants were issued for their arrest—but the men had long since gone into hiding, citing fears that they would be assassinated if they spent any more time in prison in Colombia. The reality was that they had already left Colombia.

Their presence in Colombia had caused great upset at home, where it was claimed that the IRA had been providing vital training in urban warfare tactics in exchange for financial payments—some estimated the payment from FARC's income derived from drug cartels at as much as $1m to $6m.

Coming as it did after the embarrassing exposure of an IRA gunrunning scam in Florida, the South American operation created further and perhaps even deeper problems for the republican movement as it appeared to alienate American supporters who viewed the socialist policies espoused by left-wing FARC terrorists with utter disdain.

It was a damaging episode.

Fundraisers for Sinn Féin in the United States suddenly found that wealthy American businessmen who had previously supported the party throughout the Irish peace process were now reluctant to be associated with anyone linked to what the United States viewed as the drug-running left wing socialists in FARC.

The US government had for some years been funding the Colombian government in an undeclared war on the damaging multi-million dollar drug trade from the South American country.

The path to peace in Ireland was seldom smooth. But the Colombian episode ensured yet another crisis on both sides of the Atlantic.

At first Sinn Féin denied that the three were in any way representing the republican movement, although later there was to be a considerable amount of backtracking from this position.

It didn't help the republicans when the Cuban authorities

identified Connolly as Sinn Féin's man in Havana. The eventual establishment of the 'Free the Colombia Three' movement was seen as confirmation of the republican movement's ties to the three men.

The Colombian military claimed the three republicans were posing as journalists and when intercepted on their way home they were found to have traces of explosives and drugs on their persons. As it happened, these claims were highly contentious and appeared to be politically inspired by the right wing Colombian military, which at the time was deeply upset by the direction the government was taking.

President Pastrana's peace strategy was to talk to the FARC guerillas in search of a resolution of the conflict that had lasted four decades and had witnessed tens of thousands of deaths. Pastrana's army generals wanted all-out war and seemed intent on causing the President as much embarrassment as they could to try to encourage him to abandon the talks.

Such was the magnitude of the story of three Irish republicans being arrested in Colombia, UTV decided to send a team to the South American country to try to find out what was going on. I was asked to travel with Dr Justin O'Brien, editor of the UTV *Insight* current affairs programme, and experienced cameraman Blane Scott.

This was to be a journey of discovery and it didn't take us long to find out that the FARC guerrillas met with what they described to us as representatives of the IRA. And it didn't take long to establish that the Colombian peace process was under severe distress, which pitched the government of the day against the generals in charge of the nation's regular army.

It was an explosive internal conflict which did have some bearing on the manner in which the Irishmen were intercepted and denounced so dramatically by the Colombian army generals keen to embarrass the peace strategy of President Pastrana.

President Pastrana had attempted to help push the FARC guerrillas towards a peaceful settlement by ceding control of an area the size of Switzerland to the south of Bogotá. It was to this area that the three Irishmen had travelled. We were now about to follow in their footsteps.

From Bogotá we flew south to Florencia. We then made our way to San Vicente del Coquan by road. When I say 'road', I mean a road that was once tarmac but was now pockmarked with large potholes that necessitated the driver zig-zagging around them at speed.

There was a small airport at San Vicente that had been used by the three republicans but we couldn't get a flight there—leaving us to travel by car in the company of a translator. Not long after leaving Florencia airport we were stopped at a checkpoint. Our translator explained that this was a Colombian Army checkpoint.

A few miles on we entered the ceded territory and encountered further checkpoints. But these were FARC checkpoints. It was difficult to tell the difference. FARC wore the same khaki-coloured army camouflage fatigues as the regular soldiers, although close up you could see that some of those holding weapons were very young . . . barely teenagers in fact, both boys and girls.

Our translator told us we could generally tell the difference by the quality of the footwear. Regular soldiers wore leather boots whereas the FARC guerrillas had Wellington boots.

The peasants' revolution has come a long way in four decades . . . but to the regular army generals and soldiers, the sight of what they regarded as FARC terrorists controlling a large area of Colombia was a horrifying spectacle. They regarded FARC rebels as terrorists to be confronted and killed . . . not to be pandered to by President Pastrana's peace strategy that brought political dialogue, not war, into rebel-held rainforests.

After an overnight stop at San Vicente, we then drove further south into the jungle to find a surreal image of the Colombian peace negotiations—FARC guerrillas engaging government officials in dialogue with their guns *on* the table . . . not *under* the table as unionists back home accused Sinn Féin.

The contrast with what was going on back home was inescapable. Here in Colombia, government spokesmen were escorted and protected by armed rebels as the talks were transmitted live on television from the middle of the rebels' jungle stronghold—the area ceded to them by the President as a safe haven.

To the Colombian army generals, political debate was the soft option to the military might of all-out war against rebels fighting for a Marxist cause.

FARC were keen to provide Irish television viewers with pictures of their camps where, on one occasion, we were invited to film an event to celebrate the rights of children. We watched as children played and sang songs surrounded by young people in FARC uniforms with their weapons holstered as they stood guard. But to Colombian military chiefs this kind of display inside the rebel-controlled zone was little more than propaganda.

To FARC, it was an opportunity to educate the next generation of guerrilla fighters—for the reality was that while the rebels and government talked peace, they were still very much at war. The Colombian peace process was at the time still very fragile.

As the televised talks continued, we sought out one of the FARC leaders—eventually getting to him after a number of protracted negotiations involving our excellent translator and a series of uniformed and armed rebels.

Raul Reyes described himself as a FARC commander. He explained the surreal television drama taking place a few yards away:

> We are having talks in the middle of the war. It is only here in the area of these 42,000 kilometres that we do not have military action, but outside here there are armed confrontations all around the country in which the only dead are Colombians.

Whilst we were at FARC headquarters, the Colombian military claimed victory in bloody clashes two hundreds miles north . . . the rebels' rifles no match for the image-enhancing night-sights fitted to the military's helicopter gunships. At least thirty rebels died for the loss of five soldiers.

But the Colombian authorities regarded the arrest of what it viewed as an IRA engineering team as proof that FARC's abilities to bring the war into cities was much more potent.

The arrest of the three IRA suspects undermined the Colombian government's position while strengthening that of its military.

This is how FARC's Raul Reyes viewed it all:

> The damage is that they [the Colombian military] want to cast a shadow of doubt on the two processes. But these two processes are of utmost importance to the people in both Ireland and Colombia. They want to involve the IRA and FARC in illegal activities that they are not involved in. They want to link them with drug trafficking and to put into question the peace processes initiated by the two governments. It is very bad in that sense. Furthermore, these men are being held responsible for actions that they have not done.

What was significant about our meeting with Reyes was that while the IRA and Sinn Féin back home were still in denial, he was prepared to confirm the visit of the three Irishmen on behalf of the IRA. This is what he told us:

> The first contact with the IRA was in fact this visit. Never before had we had contact with them. We were doing a political exchange comparing the peace process involving the governments of Ireland and England with ours.
>
> We consider this to be a fruitful experience for both sides. They came here as political representatives from their organisation. That was their role here, and that was the line of our exchange.

But the FARC commander was less forthcoming when asked how the Irishmen spent five weeks inside the ceded zone. He then said:

> I do not know for how long they stayed. I talked to them, we exchanged our views on both our peace processes. I do not know the length of time, that is the government's version and they know why they are talking about that length of time.

FARC of course had its own agenda, and its longstanding links with international terrorist groups is not something it wants to publicise. However, seasoned observers of the Colombian peace process advised caution. One former peace commissioner who was forced into exile because of death threats from right wing paramilitaries opposed to the process said the arrests of the Irishmen was a remarkable coincidence that suited hawkish interests in Colombia. Daniel Garcia Pena told me: 'In Colombia unfortunately there is a track record of misinformation, spectacular events are not stood up but the damage already done.'

The arrests of the three Irishmen coincided with the imminent decision on the future of the ceded zone. President Pastrana's room for manoeuvre was significantly weakened. And with presidential elections looming it was clear that the arrests fed into domestic Colombian politics.

What we did find out was that from the very beginning this was a military operation. McAuley and Monaghan were followed by undercover soldiers from the moment they arrived in Bogotá. The authorities in the capital had been briefed by international security agencies that FARC and the smaller rebel organisation, the ELN, had been in recent contact with a number of terrorist groups in Europe.

But when all three boarded an internal flight to San Vicente in the capital of the de-militarised zone, it became difficult and dangerous for the Colombian military to keep track of them where the army's writ no longer runs, and from this point on conclusive evidence of their activities is unavailable.

We took the same route as the Irishmen—the only route through an uninviting environment where even the local members of FARC constantly fight malaria and disease; it's a place you visit only if you have reason to. From San Vicente it took us over five excruciating hours driving time on barely passable primitive dirt tracks cut through the jungle. The dirt track was pockmarked with enormous craters up to six or seven feet deep and as wide as twenty feet. Often they were filled with water.

This is not a trip for tourists. We certainly did not encounter any on our journey—ten hours round trip in one day. It had to be in one day because we were under curfew back at our base in

San Vicente. We had to get home by 6 p.m.

And throughout the day we were regularly stopped and quizzed by FARC rebels. On one occasion when we stopped for refreshment at a farmhouse, we noticed a really large 4-by-4 jeep nearby and several other vehicles surrounding it. It seemed an important FARC leader was in the vicinity, but when we approached he declined our invitation to have a chat and urged us to continue on our way as quickly as possible. We didn't need to be told twice.

Foreigners making this torturous journey must have good reason to. Journalists entering the ceded zone would, I am sure, make this journey if they had reason to meet FARC leaders in the heart of the jungle territory. So 'journalism' might provide perfect cover for three republicans from Ireland travelling under false names and passports.

There is nothing here to see or to enjoy except mile after mile of dirt track roads with craters large enough to swallow up vehicles whole. There is nothing around the town of La Macarena except FARC rebels in training camps hidden in the jungle in the hills.

If you make this trip you have good reason. And at the time we were there, when it was inside the FARC-controlled zone, you could not make it without the knowledge of FARC.

At La Macarena we found no record of the Irishmen's stay there. People did not want to talk to us—or in most cases could not talk to us because of the language barrier. But with the help of our interpreter we learned that the Irishmen were likely to have spent their entire time in secret rebel camps hidden in the jungle around the town.

A Colombian newspaper published selected extracts where the Irishmen explain to the authorities their reasons for visiting. McCauley is said to have told his interrogators he came: 'First, for pleasure and also to carry out research for an Irish publication specialised in politics.'

Connolly apparently said he came as a 'tourist' who wanted to 'visit the Amazon'. When Monaghan was asked if he had met any members of FARC in San Vicente, he replied: 'No.'

What exactly the three republicans were up to in the jungles of southern Colombia remains—to this day—a matter of intense dispute . . . a dispute characterised then and now by spin and counter-spin involving British secret services, the Colombian military, FARC and Sinn Féin.

But the republicans' defence that they were merely sightseeing was comprehensively undermined by FARC, which confirmed that their visit was pre-arranged and that the three men presented themselves as the political representatives of the IRA.

Given the background of Monaghan and McAuley, it appeared that in Marxist circles at least, Chairman Mao's famous dictum that all political power grows out of the barrel of a gun remained true.

But when the three Irishmen were arrested in Bogotá after leaving the FARC stronghold, a very different interpretation was placed on their activities. The video of the suspects was released to the world media as the top generals claimed evidence of an international terrorist conspiracy. But another agenda could also be detected.

The Colombian military used the arrests as evidence that the safe haven was being abused by the FARC and that it was paying for new technology with drugs. Such accusations served to buttress the army's case for a greater share of the $1.8 billion programme of American investment designed to eradicate the drug cartels who operated with impunity throughout the Colombian countryside. British intelligence wasted no time in leaking information, which has been impossible to verify, that the IRA was testing new explosives.

What has been possible to verify is the Colombian appeal court judgement. The 144-page judgement slammed as 'naïve' and 'not credible' the explanations offered by the three Irishmen as to why they were in Colombia. It was a scathing attack on the defence put forward by the three men. The document revealed how the appeal court judges regarded with contempt the evidence offered by the three Irishmen.

Sinn Féin would say that was the kind of sentiment to be expected in a political show trial. The spectre of political interference hung over the whole Colombian episode.

—

And yet the reasons why the Irishmen were in Colombia in the first place are central to the truth of the whole controversy. I tried to get into the jail in Bogotá to see Martin McCauley—someone I had met many times years earlier whilst researching a BBC *Panorama* programme. But my approach was unsuccessful. The consequence was that no one heard the three Irishmen explain the reasons for their visit.

The Colombian appeal court judges did at least have access to tapes and transcripts of what the Irishmen had to say and they chose to de-construct the explanations given by McCauley, Monaghan and Connolly.

For a start, they took the view that Monaghan and McCauley —both of whom have terrorist convictions—were insolvent and therefore incapable of having the means to travel to Colombia under their own steam . . . as they had apparently claimed.

Imposing seventeen-year jail sentences on each of the three republicans, the judges said they were not convinced that they had the means to travel around the world, stopping off in various cities en route to Colombia.

In their judgement, and presumably on the guidance of some third party, they expressed the view that as ex-prisoners, McCauley and Monaghan had difficulty finding steady jobs in Ireland, leaving them dependent on their wives or on temporary work for a source of income.

The judges also questioned Connolly's financial means. They noted he worked in Cuba as a translator and as Sinn Féin's envoy in Havana. However, they said Connolly entered Colombia from Madrid. They asked: 'Could it be that a translator in Cuba earns enough to come to Colombia for holidays via Madrid?'

That McCauley and Monaghan travelled without having to use a travel agency to organise their trip also intrigued the judges. They thought it especially strange that Monaghan claimed he worked for Coiste na nIarchimi, an NGO in Ireland, but did not plan his trip to ensure he got back to work on time. And even more unusual, they thought, was the fact that Monaghan intended to end the trip to Colombia in Paris—a city they noted he was not of a mind to visit according to his own statements to the authorities after his arrest.

As for Monaghan's other claims that he was preparing to write an article on the Colombian peace process, the judges said he had no notes, interviews or articles to show he was conducting an investigation. He did have a video camera, but the tapes were blank and forensic examination had failed to demonstrate one way or another if they had always been blank or had been used and then erased.

The judges said: 'The absence of evidence to back up their claims makes it impossible to believe their naïve explanations— that some came over here on holidays, and the other to practise Spanish.'

They added that if Connolly really did work as a translator, he would have already been 'proficient in both languages'.

The judges went on to say:

The accused dare to say that they were there for a little more than a month without encountering a single guerrilla fighter that could have stopped their free movement in the zone, or that their entry went unnoticed and that it was the most appropriate place to spend a few days holidays.

The fact that Monaghan and Connolly had travelled to neighbouring countries in the past on false passports was viewed by the judges as being of vital importance, as it linked them to evidence from two FARC informants who had claimed to have seen the Irishmen before during previous visits.

In short, the judges reached the conclusion that the presence of the three Irishmen in Colombia was not what they claimed: 'Their explanations have been totally discredited.'

Of course there were individuals on either side of the Atlantic who did not need the Colombian appeal court judges to tell them about the 'guilt' of the three republicans.

From the outset, unionists claimed the Colombian escapade showed that the IRA and Sinn Féin were not yet ready for decommissioning . . . not yet ready to forsake violence for political progress.

The unionists were not alone.

Alarm bells rang in the United States. The gamble made by corporate America in supporting Sinn Féin suddenly seemed too high. Irish republicans were being associated with cocaine and Marxism—twin evils of American foreign policy. FARC made no apologies for its Marxist leanings and said the allegations that its enormous cash reserves come from drug trafficking were designed to justify American imperialism.

This is how FARC's Raul Reyes put it:

That is a big lie. If FARC had that money, that income, there would be a new government in Colombia. That is a huge lie. They do that to get more finance from the Plan Colombia [American aid programme to fight drug cartels], which means more war against our people and more American involvement in the domestic affairs of our country with our government's agreement.

Certainly, the Colombian military went strangely quiet on the evidence of cocaine traces on the three IRA suspects. A senior source close to the prosecutor's investigation told me: 'There were not enough traces of cocaine to even warrant a possession charge.' But the damage had been done.

The IRA itself had remained notably silent on the Colombia Three until an event that shook the world.

The September 11 attacks by al Qaeda terrorists in New York left thousands dead. This was a major terrorist assault on US soil and although it removed the Colombian story off the front pages for a long, long time, the 9/11 slaughter of so many innocent workers was a painful experience for the entire nation.

It had the effect of making individuals who had previously supported the IRA conflict in Northern Ireland think again about their contributions, financially and politically, to what the

Provisionals called the 'war' against the British. After all, there had been many instances in Ireland of innocent people becoming collateral damage in terrorist attacks.

It encouraged them to think of ending the conflict in Ireland and of pushing harder on the IRA to put away the guns and engage in dialogue.

After the 9/11 attacks, the IRA felt moved to issue this statement:

> First of all we wish to extend our sympathy to the people of the United States and especially to the families and friends of the victims of the deplorable attacks in New York, Washington and Pennsylvania.
>
> On August 8 we confirmed that the IRA leadership had agreed a scheme with the IICD (the Independent International Commission on Decommissioning) to put IRA arms completely and verifiably beyond use.
>
> This unprecedented IRA initiative was the result of lengthy discussions with the IICD over a long period. It was another expression of our willingness to enhance the peace process and it involved considerable problems for us and for our organisation.
>
> The IRA leadership's ability to speedily and substantially progress the decision was completely undermined by the setting of further preconditions and the outright rejection of the IICD statement by the Ulster Unionist Party leadership. Subsequent actions by the British government including a continued failure to fulfil its commitments, remove the conditions necessary for progress. On August 14 we withdrew our proposal.
>
> However, as an earnest of our willingness to resolve the issue of arms, the IRA leadership wish to confirm that our representative will intensify the engagement with the IICD. This dialogue is within the context of our commitment to deal satisfactorily with the question of arms. It is with a view to accelerating progress towards the comprehensive resolution of this issue.

Aerial view of the Northern Bank headquarters (circled) where £26m was stolen a few days before Christmas 2004. (*Pacemaker Press International*)

Security camera footage of Northern Bank employee Chris Ward leaving the bank with £1m in a sports bag to hand over to a member of the robbery gang in a nearby street. (*Reuters*)

Chris Ward pictured when he agreed to tell reporters about his ordeal as a hostage of the robbery gang. He was later arrested by police and charged in connection with the heist. (*Pacemaker Press International*)

The police released this CCTV footage of the white van used by the robbery gang making its way through Belfast on the night of the robbery. (*Pacemaker Press International*)

The burnt-out remains of the car used by the kidnappers of Karen McMullan, wife of Northern Bank employee Kevin. It was found not far from the forest where Mrs McMullan was eventually set free. (*Pacemaker Press International*)

Business as usual for the Northern Bank ... the morning after the bank raid cash deliveries continue during the Christmas shopping rush. (*Pacemaker Press International*)

Newspaper sellers were sitting right on top of the story the day after the raid. (*Empics*)

PSNI Assistant Chief Constable Sam Kinkaid held a news conference to release details of the bank raid. (*Pacemaker Press International*)

Police on duty at the bank entrance where raiders collected £26m in cash the previous evening. (*Reuters*)

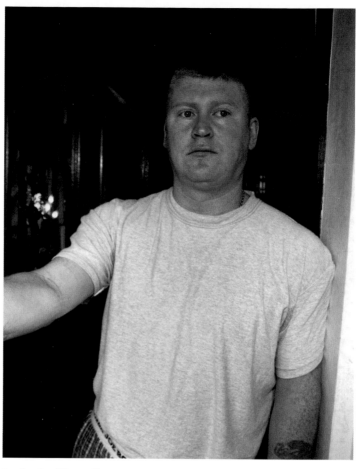

Leading Republican Eddie Copeland at his Ardoyne home. His house was one of those searched by police shortly after news broke of the raid. (*Empics*)

Graffiti Belfast style. The spelling is poor, but the message is a clear attempt to mimic the current advertising style of a famous beer. (*Reuters*)

After months of investigation, the police finally make a move. They raid a number of properties in the County Down village of Kilcoo and make a number of arrests. (*Empics*)

Detective Superintendent Andy Sproule of the PSNI, who initially headed up the investigation into the Northern Bank raid before his retirement. The police blamed the IRA for the robbery. (*Pacemaker Press International*)

A Northern Bank £20 note put on display by the bank after the robbery. The bank also announced plans to design new notes to frustrate the criminal gang involved in the robbery. (*Reuters*)

Sinn Féin councillor Tom Hanlon pictured on his release from Togher Garda Station in Cork. He was detained for questioning about the Northern Bank robbery. (*Empics*)

Police searches spread to various parts of Northern Ireland. Here officers search a pond near homes in the Tyrone village of Beragh, near Omagh. (*Empics*)

Garda forensic officers remove material from a house in the village of Farren, Co. Cork, as part of their investigations into the recovery of cash believed to be connected to the Northern Bank robbery. In all, seven people were brought in for questioning. (*Reuters*)

Company director Ted Cunningham leaves the Bridewell Garda Station after questioning about links to the Northern Bank robbery. A Garda search of his County Cork home found over £2m in sterling bank notes concealed in a wheelie-bin.
(*Empics*)

The Newforge sports club used by members of the PSNI was the setting for a bizarre discovery—£50,000 worth of stolen Northern Bank notes were hidden in the ceiling of a lavatory. (*Reuters*)

Hugh Orde, the Chief Constable of the PSNI, who said the IRA was responsible for the Northern Bank robbery. (*Empics*)

The former head of Scotland Yard's anti-terrorism squad, John Grieve, is a member of the Independent Monitoring Commission. The IMC, like the police, blamed the IRA for the £26m raid on the Northern Bank. (*Reuters*)

Sinn Féin's chief negotiator Martin McGuinness addresses a news conference in January 2005 telling reporters that the IRA was not involved in the Northern Bank raid. (*Reuters*)

Sinn Féin Assembly members protest at Stormont over the IMC's report linking the IRA to the Northern Bank robbery. (*AFP/Getty*)

Progress will be directly influenced by the attitude of other parties to the peace process, including and especially, the British government. The IRA's commitment is without question.

However, as we have said before, peace making and peace keeping is a collective effort. It is our considered view that the Irish peace process can succeed. The continued failure or refusal to sustain the political process and to deliver real and meaningful change has a direct bearing on how this will be accomplished.

The IRA has contributed consistently and in a meaningful way to the creation of a climate which would facilitate the search for a durable settlement. We will continue to do so, including through our engagement with the IICD, particularly at this difficult time, and in the period immediately ahead.

We also wish to state our attitude to the arrests of three Irishmen in Colombia. There has been a lot of ill-founded and mischievous speculation about these arrests and some ill-considered and aggressive comment directed at our organisation.

We wish to make it clear that the Army Council sent no one to Colombia to train or to engage in any military cooperation with any group. The IRA has not interfered in the internal affairs of Colombia and will not so do. The IRA is not a threat to the peace process in Ireland or in Colombia. The three men have asserted their support for the process and we accept that.

The statement was signed, 'P. O'Neill, Irish Republican Publicity Bureau, Dublin.'

But the damage done by the arrests of the Colombia Three continued to plague the republican peace movement for many years. The prolonged process of investigation brought regular publicity and then, of course, there was the high-profile republican campaign to bring the three men home.

Now here it was, in December 2004, hitting the front pages once again.

The story represented another embarrassing episode for the IRA and Sinn Féin, coming as it did in the weeks after a row had erupted in the Republic over plans by Taoiseach Bertie Ahern to release those already serving jail sentences for the murder of Garda McCabe.

And of course the IRA had also denied involvement in the murder of Garda McCabe. Such denials had become a regular feature in the republican vocabulary ever since the cessation of hostilities in the nineties.

Now things were about to become even worse.

But as readers pored over the pages of the *Sunday World* on 19 December, the Northern Bank gang was about to inflict further pain on the peace process.

That night, as the Sinn Féin hierarchy prepared for bed, having spent the day analysing the Sunday papers to help them work out their strategies for the week ahead, members of the robbery gang were moving into position—taking over two homes of bank staff and moving men and weapons into position to make the raid a success.

The robbers were on the eve of an event that would once again put the entire future of the peace process and a power-sharing government in the balance.

Of course, the peace process was already terminally ill— pushed to the brink of extinction by the last-minute row a few weeks earlier over a photographic record of IRA decommissioning.

The idea of photographic evidence of the act of putting IRA weapons beyond use was apparently first floated at Leeds Castle in Kent in September 2004. The British and Irish Prime Ministers said they believed it was an ideal solution to the problem of verification. The proposal was that the pictures would not be published until the power-sharing Executive had been restored.

It was claimed that Gerry Adams and his team accepted this plan in principle. But if they did, it would appear that as political agreement with the DUP approached, the IRA decided it was not acceptable.

In the week before the robbery, the blame game focused on

who was responsible for failure to nail down the agreement that
would restore devolved government at Stormont.

Sinn Féin said the idea of a photograph had been raised at the
last minute. Ian Paisley said otherwise.

But the IRA's refusal to accept photographic evidence of their
decommissioning efforts meant that even if there was a
destruction of all their weapons, it would count for nothing
unless it was photographed.

In early December the IRA issued a lengthy statement to
explain why it was not prepared to agree to the photograph. The
statement, published here in full, also dealt with the most recent
proposals from the British and Irish governments for a
comprehensive agreement.

The is what the IRA said:

More than ten years ago, an IRA cessation publicly heralded
the onset of the Irish peace process. Since then, the IRA has,
time and again, demonstrated its commitment to sustaining
and developing that process through a series of very
significant and substantive initiatives.

In the context of the work to conclude a comprehensive
agreement, the leadership of Óglaigh na hÉireann decided:

• to support a comprehensive agreement by moving into a
new mode which reflects our determination to see the
transition to a totally peaceful society

• all IRA Volunteers be given specific instructions not to
engage in any activity which might thereby endanger that
new agreement

• the IRA leadership also decided that we will, in this context,
conclude the process to completely and verifiably put all
our arms beyond use

• we instructed our representative to agree with the IICD the
completion of this process, speedily, and if possible by the
end of December

• to further enhance public confidence we agreed to the
presence of two clergymen as observers during this
process.

The IRA leadership decided to contribute in this way to a comprehensive agreement to resolve all outstanding issues, including those of concern within unionism. For his part, Ian Paisley demanded that our contribution be photographed, and reduced to an act of humiliation.

This was never possible. Knowing this, he made this demand publicly as the excuse for his rejection of an overall agreement to create a political context with the potential to remove the causes of conflict. As the IRA leadership has said before, this is a context in which Irish republicans and unionists can, as equals, pursue our respective political objectives peacefully.

We restate our commitment to the peace process. But we will not submit to a process of humiliation.

We commend our Volunteers and the wider republican base for their patience and discipline in these testing times. Our commitment, like theirs, to our republican objectives is undiminished.

We thank those who have made genuine contributions to the efforts to find solutions to ongoing problems. While acknowledging these efforts, we reiterate our view that progress cannot be made by pandering to the demands of those who are against change.

The search for a just and lasting peace is a challenging one. The IRA leadership has risen to that challenge. The British Government and the leaders of unionism must do likewise.

So there was no deal. The IRA viewed the DUP's demands as an attempt to humiliate them.

The only certainty was that this last minute failure to secure a historic deal between sworn enemies had produced yet another political stalemate. And as the political fallout from the bank raid continued, worse was to follow.

What happened in a Belfast bar on the night of 30 January 2005 was going to ignite an issue about criminality that the IRA would find difficult to shake off—an issue over murder that would attract international contempt for the whole republican movement.

Thirty-three-year-old Robert McCartney was enjoying a drink in Magennis's Whiskey Café. The bar's entrance overlooks the rear of the building housing the Royal Courts of Justice. On weekdays the pub serves up lunches to lawyers and court officials, but this was a Sunday night and at weekends the clientele mainly comes from the nearby communities at Short Strand and the Markets. Also in the bar was a group of IRA men and a number of members of Sinn Féin returning from a Bloody Sunday commemoration.

There was an incident as Robert McCartney and his friend Brendan Devine sipped their pints of stout. One of the IRA men thought McCartney or Devine were laughing over what he thought was a 'slight' or a lewd joke directed at his girlfriend. Insults were shouted across the bar.

Apparently, Devine attempted to smooth things over. A drink proffered to the woman in question was accepted, but the IRA man was demanding an apology, which was not forthcoming.

Tempers did not calm. A fight broke out. Devine was attacked inside the bar. He received throat injuries from a broken bottle. In fact his throat was cut and his stomach cut open.

McCartney took Devine out of the bar and called a taxi. But then the two men were set upon by a group of men who followed them out of the bar. Some estimates said fifteen to twenty men were involved, although others said it was more like four or five.

In any event, they outnumbered their prey. McCartney and Devine were forced up an entry at the side of the bar and were beaten and kicked. McCartney was kicked repeatedly in the head and allegedly had an eye gouged out. He was also stabbed repeatedly.

Both men were left for dead. No ambulance was called. The attackers went back inside the bar. What happened next was crucial. The attackers and their friends, including some females, destroyed forensic evidence inside the pub. Just like the Northern

Bank raiders, the bar room killers were forensically aware. They used disinfectant to remove all possible forensic traces. The bar's security videos were removed.

Police officers found the two men some time later and took them to hospital. Robert McCartney survived the night but died the next morning at daylight. He had lived with his partner Bridgeen Hagans, the mother of his two sons—Brandon, aged two and Conlead, four. They had plans to marry in the summer of 2005.

In spite of the fact that there were at least seventy people in the bar, the police could find no one to tell them what had happened.

Robert McCartney's five sisters knew more about what happened than the officers investigating the case. The sisters—Gemma, Paula, Donna, Catherine and Claire—were also quickly aware of who was involved in the fracas that led to their brother's murder.

Even more disturbing for them was the knowledge in their own community that the IRA men involved had warned everyone in the bar to remain silent about what they had seen and were now active in the area making it clear that no one was to co-operate with the police.

The sisters—republicans from the Short Strand area and Sinn Féin supporters—were not prepared to accept that in times of peace the IRA could dish out its own brand of justice and then impose themselves on the people they had once claimed to safeguard during the conflict.

The IRA men in Short Strand under-estimated the determination of Robert McCartney's sisters and his partner, Bridgeen. They apparently did not foresee that there would be an uprising against this arrogant demonstration of power. There was a spontaneous outpouring of support for the McCartney families.

After the funeral, Bridgeen and the sisters went on local radio to make a plea for witnesses. Public demonstrations were well attended as the McCartney family began their crusade for justice. They were demanding that the IRA stop intimidating witnesses and that the IRA make those involved in the murder give themselves up. They also accused the IRA of covering up for the killers.

The IRA was compelled to listen to what was being said in the name of many in the Short Strand community and issued a statement on 15 February, two weeks after the McCartney murder:

> The IRA was not involved in the brutal killing of Robert McCartney. It has been reported that people are being intimidated or prevented from assisting the McCartney family in their search for truth and justice. We wish to make it absolutely clear that no one should hinder or impede the McCartney family in their search for truth and justice. Anyone who can help the family in this should do so. Those who were involved must take responsibility for their own actions which run contrary to republican ideals.

The McCartney family saw no benefit coming from the IRA statement. In fact, they saw for themselves the kind of intimidation that was keeping the truth from reaching the courts. They had to face the men they believed were responsible for Robert's death every day as they went about their business— mourning the loss of a very popular brother and father.

Sinn Féin found the going tough in an area where they had always been welcome. Party members were heckled in the streets of Short Strand—once by an uncle of the dead man in front of television cameras.

Coming so soon after the Northern Bank heist, the McCartney murder placed the focus of the world once again on Sinn Féin and the IRA.

Sinn Féin was being challenged to say whether this was the kind of law and order they envisaged for the future? They were also being challenged to help the McCartney family find justice. But as the party hadn't yet signed up to the new policing arrangements in the North, it was caught between a rock and a hard place.

Publicly Gerry Adams and other leading Sinn Féin members

were advocating that anyone with information about the brutal murder of Robert McCartney should come forward and tell their story ... just not to the investigating police officers.

As the McCartney campaign grew in stature, creating enormous interest worldwide, the IRA was compelled to issue another statement on 25 February. This one followed an internal investigation and it is reproduced here in full:

> Following our investigation the IRA leadership, along with the leadership of the Belfast Command, initiated disciplinary proceedings through Court Martial. This was in accordance with IRA Standing Orders. These proceedings were directed only against IRA Volunteers.
>
> The outcome of the Courts Martial include the dismissal of three Volunteers, two of whom were high ranking Volunteers. One of these Volunteers had already gone to a solicitor immediately after the incident to make a statement of his actions on that night. The other two were advised in the strongest terms possible to come forward and to take responsibility for their actions, as the McCartney family have asked.
>
> In our statement of February 15th, we made it absolutely clear that no one should hinder or impede the McCartney family in their search for truth and justice and that anyone who could help them in that search should do so.
>
> A dispute broke out between a senior republican and a group of people that included Robert McCartney and Brendan Devine after an initial heated verbal exchange between the senior republican and Robert McCartney. At that point another man and the senior republican were involved in a further heated exchange. Blows were exchanged and a major melee erupted in the bar.
>
> Neither that man nor the senior republican had weapons of any description in their possession though both were struck with bottles thrown by others. Robert McCartney played no part in the melee. Both Brendan Devine and the senior republican received serious stab wounds inside the bar.

A crowd spilled out onto the street. Verbal abuse and threats were being shouted by many of those present.

Some of those at the scene, including some republicans, tried to calm the situation. The senior republican's wounds were tended by people at the scene and he was quickly taken to hospital.

In the meantime Brendan Devine, Robert McCartney and another man ended up in Market Street. It is the view of our investigation that these men were leaving the scene.

They were followed into Market Street where Robert McCartney and Brendan Devine were attacked and stabbed. Both men were stabbed by the same man. Robert McCartney died a short time later in hospital. No materials under the control of or belonging to the IRA were produced or used at any time during this savage attack.

A member of the bar staff was threatened by an individual who then took the CCTV tape away and destroyed it. Those at the scene are responsible for the clean-up or destruction of evidence at the scene. There should be no misunderstanding of our position in that regard. Any intimidation or threats in the name of the IRA or otherwise to any person who wishes to help the McCartney family will not be tolerated.

The internal disciplinary steps taken by the IRA are a matter for the IRA. They are not intended to be, nor should they be, seen as a substitute for the requests of the McCartney family. IRA volunteers fully understand that they are bound by rules and regulations and a Code of Conduct. There will be no tolerance of anyone who steps outside of these rules, regulations or code. Anyone who brings the IRA into disrepute will be held accountable.

It would appear the IRA managed to get information out of those they interviewed—many of them had offered themselves through solicitors for interview by police but had adopted the tried and tested IRA anti-interrogation method of staring blankly at the walls in silence.

And on the basis of their internal investigation the IRA had kicked out three members. And yet, according to members of the McCartney family, these same individuals were still free to roam around the Short Strand area enforcing the silence of those who had stories to tell about the events on 30 January.

There's no doubt the murder of Robert McCartney was brutal and an affront all civilised people. The trouble for Sinn Féin was that the McCartney family—their supporters and voters—were not going to accept the despicable attempt by the IRA to cover up the murder.

There was no way the family would settle for anything less than justice and for them that meant having the guilty parties in court. Not just the person who stabbed Robert but all those engaged in the clean-up and the subsequent cover-up.

Publicly Sinn Féin adopted the position of telling those present in the bar to come forward with their information to help the McCartney family get justice. Of course, the party did not recommend going to the police because at this stage of the peace process the new police force, the PSNI, was not acceptable to republicans.

The IRA claimed publicly that it urged those involved in Robert McCartney's murder to take responsibility for their actions to help the family of the dead man get justice. But they did not recommend going to the police.

Both Sinn Féin and the IRA knew the McCartney family wanted people made accountable in court. This was not a murder sanctioned by the IRA leadership as part of the 'war' against British occupation. No, this was a grubby act of barbaric criminality that threw the whole republican movement into a major quandary. If there was to be justice, there had to be a prosecution. And if there was to be a prosecution, there had to be co-operation from eyewitnesses with the police who investigate murder and crime and gather evidence for court hearings.

But did Sinn Féin or the IRA urge people to go to the police? No. How exactly did they see justice being done? They knew what had to be done to provide justice for the McCartney family, but it stuck in their craw to have to say it out loud and in public.

So anyone coming forward was expected to go to a solicitor,

rather than to the police.

Some witnesses did come forward for questioning by the police but simply were not prepared to sign their names to their statements for fear of reprisals. No sworn statements to help prosecute the guilty.

Then of course there was the problem of Sinn Féin members who were in the bar and who witnessed the terrible events unfold there. The party had to hold its own inquiry and for a time as many as seven party members were suspended pending the outcome of those investigations.

Last but not least, there was the attitude of the IRA. People in Short Strand who had always been supportive of the IRA as defenders of their community were not now as supportive of an organisation which was seen to be engaged in a cover-up to protect brutal killers—some of them still members of the organisation.

There were now people turning against the organisation. How could it allow the killers of Robert McCartney to walk around freely? People were not prepared to live with these killers in their midst. That's why there was so much support for the McCartney family and Bridgeen.

Perhaps the most frightening thought was that this was the way the Provos viewed justice in the new peace. If so, it was a terrifying prospect few wanted to accept.

Sinn Féin could see that this situation had the potential to damage their vote.

As for the IRA's very public denouncement of the murder and the cover-up, there was no let-up in the intimidation of potential witnesses. The killers still walked about the Short Strand.

It wasn't long before the three expelled IRA men were identified in the press. On 27 February, the *Sunday World* named the three men as:
- former Short Strand Provo heavy James Gerard Davison, nicknamed 'Big Jock'
- ex-OC of the IRA in the nearby Markets, Jim McCormick, known as 'Dim'
- and another prominent Provo, Gerard Montgomery

The paper quoted a statement from the McCartney sisters which said: 'We confirm that we believe the three being named in the *Sunday World* are central to Robert's murder inquiry. We also believe they are the three thrown out of the IRA.'

But the three expelled IRA members continued to stalk the streets of the Short Strand. And even more remarkable is that in spite of the expulsions, leading IRA commander Bobby Storey was seen on the streets of Short Strand with Davison.

It was an act designed to send a chilling message to the people of the area . . . that Davison was still very much in with the Provos.

The McCartney family kept up the pressure for what they called justice. They wanted Robert's killers before the courts. As they continued their campaign, the IRA sought a meeting. Apparently, the IRA offered to shoot those responsible for Robert's murder. The McCartney family declined. They wanted no one killed. They wanted justice.

The IRA issued yet another statement in early March. This third statement gave more information about the Provisionals' own investigation. Here it is in full:

Representatives of Óglaigh na hÉireann met with Bridgeen Hagans, the partner of Robert McCartney, and with his sisters before our statement of 25 February was issued. The meeting lasted five-and-a-half hours. During this time the IRA representatives gave the McCartney family a detailed account of our investigation.

Our investigation found that after the initial melee in Magennis's bar, a crowd spilled out on to the street and Robert McCartney, Brendan Devine and two other men were pursued into Market Street. Four men were involved in the attacks in Market Street on the evening of 30 January. A fifth person was at the scene. He took no part in the attacks and was responsible for moving to safety one of the two people accompanying Robert McCartney and Brendan Devine.

One man was responsible for providing the knife that was used in the stabbing of Robert McCartney and Brendan

ANNUS HORRIBILIS   119

Devine in Market Street. He got the knife from the kitchen of
Magennis's Bar. Another man stabbed Robert McCartney and
Brendan Devine. A third man kicked and beat Robert
McCartney after he had been stabbed in Market Street. A
fourth man hit a friend of Robert McCartney and Brendan
Devine across the face with a steel bar in Market Street.

The man who provided the knife also retrieved it from the
scene and destroyed it. The same man also took the CCTV tape
from the bar, after threatening a member of staff, and later
destroyed it. He also burned clothes after the attack.

Reports in the media have alleged that up to 12 IRA
Volunteers were involved in the events in Market Street. Our
investigation found that this is not so. Of the four people
directly involved in the attacks in Market Street, two were IRA
Volunteers. The other two were not. The IRA knows the
identity of all these men.

The build-up to the attack and stabbings was also outlined
to the family and subsequently set out publicly in the IRA's
statement of 25 February. The IRA representatives detailed the
outcome of the internal disciplinary proceedings thus far, and
stated in clear terms that the IRA was prepared to shoot the
people directly involved in the killing of Robert McCartney.

The McCartney family raised their concerns with the IRA
representatives. These included: Firstly, the family made it
clear that they did not want physical action taken against
those involved. They stated that they wanted those individuals
to give a full account of their actions in court.

Secondly, they raised concerns about the intimidation of
witnesses. The IRA's position on this was set out in
unambiguous and categoric terms on February 15 and
February 25. Before and after this meeting with the family, the
IRA gave direct assurances on their safety to three named
individuals who the family believe were the targets of
intimidation.

Since we met the family, at that time, the good offices of an
independent third party have been employed to reinforce
these assurances with two of the three men. To this point, the

third party has not been able to contact the other man. We have urged any witnesses who can assist in any way to come forward. That remains our position. The only interest the IRA has in this case is to see truth and justice achieved.

Since we issued our statement on February 25 there has been much political and media comment on what we had to say. Predictably, our opponents and enemies who have their own agendas have used this brutal killing to attack republicans and to advance their own narrow political interests. The public will make their own judgment on this. We sought and held a second meeting with the McCartney family in the presence of an independent observer.

In the course of this we reiterated our position in respect of witnesses, including our view that all witnesses should come forward. We also revisited details of the incident. We disclosed the following to the family: The conclusions of the IRA's investigations are based on voluntary admissions by those involved. The names of those involved in the attacks and stabbings of Robert McCartney, Brendan Devine and the assault on another man in Market Street were given to the family.

This included the names of the two men responsible for providing the knife, using the knife, destroying the knife, destroying the CCTV tape and burning clothes. In addition, we informed the family that: We have ordered anyone who was present on the night to go forward and to give a full and honest account of their actions. That includes those who have already been subject to the IRA's internal disciplinary proceedings.

We are continuing to press all of those involved in the events around the killings of Robert McCartney to come forward. The IRA is setting out all of the above at length because it is important that those issues of truth and justice are successfully resolved. We are doing our best to work with the family and to respect their wishes.

The McCartney family responded to this statement by issuing

one of their own. Robert's sister Claire read out the following to reporters:

> The investigation by the IRA in the murder of Robert is a matter for themselves. For this family it would only be in court, where transparency and accountability prevail, that justice will be done.
>
> It is the family's position that up to 12 Volunteers were involved in the cover-up, not the offence in Market Street where up to three were involved. However, it was that cover-up which prevented those who murdered Robert from being brought to justice.
>
> We met with the IRA at their request on Monday, 5 March. During that meeting we were informed of the findings of their investigation to date, but again it is only in a court that the truth will come out. At the meeting Bridgeen [Hagans, Robert's partner] asked the IRA representatives a question that has been haunting her and the family for five weeks: why did they kill Robert?
>
> They responded openly and directly that there was no reason. We want the investigation into Robert's murder to be conducted through due process. Only this will ensure people are held to account for their actions.
>
> It is now five weeks since Robert was murdered and no one has come forward with substantial evidence. This must be due to ongoing intimidation and fear. Until they do we will continue to campaign for justice for Robert.

Yet, in spite of the strongly worded IRA statements warning against intimidation of witnesses, it continued.

Meanwhile, the McCartney family's campaign for justice struck a chord that took them on a journey of discovery. They found themselves the focus of international media attention. They had meetings with politicians, with heads of government throughout Europe and even with the President of the United States, when they were invited to the White House for the St Patrick's Day celebrations.

Their visit to America came at a time when Sinn Féin was not invited to any US government events to mark St Patrick's Day. Normally Gerry Adams would be in Washington to curry favour and gain vital funding for Sinn Féin.

But as an indication of how displeased Irish America was about the Colombia Three, the Northern Bank raid and the McCartney murder, Sinn Féin was excluded. Of course, no Northern Ireland politicians were invited but there was a strong sense of outrage at the IRA's ongoing criminality.

The US Special Envoy to Northern Ireland, Mitchell Reiss, met the McCartney family and said the US administration was doing all in its power to help them. The family also held talks with US Senator Ted Kennedy, who had refused to meet Gerry Adams during the Sinn Féin leader's St Patrick's week trip to the US. A spokeswoman for Senator Kennedy said he had cancelled a meeting because of the IRA's 'ongoing criminal activity'.

Also present at the White House to offer the McCartney family support was Ann McCabe, the widow of Garda Jerry McCabe who was shot dead by the IRA during a robbery in the Irish Republic in 1996. She said she supported the McCartney family's quest for justice.

The Taoiseach Bertie Ahern presented President Bush with a bowl of shamrock at the White House St Patrick's Day reception. He said the Irish government was as fully committed as in 1998 to making the Good Friday Agreement work and knew they could count on President Bush's continued support. He said inclusive government in Northern Ireland was only possible when there was 'definitive closure to paramilitary capability and activity including all forms of criminality'.

The fact that the Irish government had earlier gone on record to say it believed Gerry Adams and Martin McGuinness were members of the IRA Army Council simply underlined how isolated the party had become since the turn of the year.

Meanwhile, Gerry Adams said the McCartney murder case had become steeped in politics. He said the only people who could not be accused of political motivation were the McCartney family themselves.

The continuing isolation of the republican movement in Dublin was another source of great discomfort to Sinn Féin. As St Patrick's Day approached there was a statement from the killers of Garda Jerry McCabe. All attempts to have them freed under the terms of the Good Friday Agreement had failed and it had become a thorn in the side of the peace process for republicans.

This is what they had to say:

> We deeply regret the death of Garda Jerry McCabe and the wounding of Garda Ben O'Sullivan during an IRA operation in Adare in June 1996. We deeply regret and apologise for this and the hurt and grief we have caused to their families. There was never any intent to attack any members of the Garda Siochána.
>
> We are qualifying IRA prisoners under the Good Friday Agreement. This has been confirmed by the High Court and the Supreme Court. The Irish Government have an obligation to release us. They have refused to do so and are now presenting our release as an obstacle to negotiations and an agreement. For this reason we do not want our release to be part of any further negotiations with the Irish government. We are totally committed to the peace process. We will not allow ourselves to be used as political pawns or hostages to undermine this process. The cause of lasting peace is too important.

The statement was issued to RTÉ by Kevin Walsh, Pearse McAuley, Jeremiah Sheehy and Michael O'Neill on 13 March 2005.

There's no doubt Sinn Féin were having to work hard to regain some confidence with both the British and Irish governments and in the United States as well. Their greatest fear was the loss of political clout which would result from the increasingly loud cries of criminality directed at the IRA.

Ever since the Northern Bank robbery, the IRA had been closely scrutinised by the British and Irish governments. The increased frequency of IRA statements was an indication of the discomfort being experienced by the whole Provisional movement. Perhaps what really stung the IRA was the fact that the two governments had chosen to turn a blind eye to so much of their criminal enterprise in the previous couple of years.

The deafening government silence over these criminal activities created the mindset among republicans that it could continue without any political ramifications for them or the peace process. However, it seems that taking £26m of cash from the Northern Bank was a step too far. The timing and scale of the robbery did suddenly have an impact on the political landscape.

Now with the murder of Robert McCartney, the pressure was intensified on Sinn Féin. The governments had removed their gloves and very quickly the sins of the IRA's recent past were quickly quantified and publicly listed. IRA involvement in criminal activity was not confined to Northern Ireland but stretched into Dublin as well.

Sinn Féin attempted to redress the balance by inviting Bridgeen Hagans and the McCartney sisters to attend the party conference in Dublin. They accepted and received an ovation from more than 1,000 delegates.

Soon afterwards came the IRA Easter message. Again the whole issue of criminality was addressed. Here's what they had to say:

> On this, the 89th anniversary of the Easter Rising of 1916, we remember the men and women of every generation who have given their lives in the struggle for Irish freedom.
>
> The leadership of Óglaigh na hÉireann extends solidarity to the families of our comrades who have fallen during this phase of the struggle. We remember those comrades with honour and pride. We send solidarity to our Volunteers and to our friends and supporters at home and abroad. We think of our imprisoned comrades and their families at this time also.
>
> Over ten years ago, the leadership of the IRA declared a complete cessation of military operations. We did so to enhance the development of the Irish peace process. From then until now we have, on a number of occasions, demonstrated our continuing support for this process.

At times of significant crisis or political impasse, we have taken initiatives to move the situation forward. Our approach has been premised on the belief that the achievement of a just and lasting peace requires constant forward momentum in the peace process. For the past two years, the peace process has been locked in stalemate and has slipped backwards into deepening crisis.

During that period, specifically in October 2003 and in December 2004, we agreed to significant initiatives as part of an agreement to break the logjam. On each occasion, other parties reneged on their commitments. An unprecedented opportunity to transform the situation on the island of Ireland was thrown away by rejectionist unionism, aided and abetted by the two governments.

The DUP attempted to turn the initiative of December 2004 into a humiliation of the IRA. The concerted efforts of both governments since then to undermine the integrity of our cause, by seeking to criminalise the republican struggle, is clear evidence that our opponents remain fixated with the objective of defeating republicans rather than developing the peace process.

The sustained campaign directed against the republican people over recent months is nothing new. We have seen and heard it all before. Those who opted to follow the Thatcher path will not succeed. Our patriot dead are not criminals. We are not criminals.

Republican men and women suffered deprivation and torture to defeat attempts to criminalise our struggle. Ten of our comrades endured the agony of hunger strike and died defeating the criminalisation strategy. We will not betray their courage by tolerating criminality within our own ranks. We will not allow our opponents to further their own petty self-interests by levelling false allegations against Óglaigh na hÉireann.

The IRA has spelt out its position in relation to the killing of Robert McCartney. It was wrong, it was murder, it was a crime. But it was not carried out by the IRA, nor was it carried

out on behalf of the IRA. The IRA moved quickly to deal with
those involved. We have tried to assist in whatever way we can.
Unfortunately, it would appear that no matter what we do, it
will never be enough for some.

Those in the political and media establishments who have
been so quick to jump on the bandwagon have again laid bare
their own hypocrisy. This causes justifiable resentment
among republicans. But it must not cloud the issue. Óglaigh
na hÉireann expects the highest standards of conduct from
our Volunteers. Struggle requires sacrifice and discipline, it
promises hardship and suffering. Our fallen comrades rose to
those challenges and met them head on.

The discipline and commitment of our Volunteers and the
wider republican base have been the backbone of our
struggle. In these testing times, that steadfastness and
determination are needed more and more. We salute you and
urge you to remain strong and united. The crisis in the peace
process and the reinvigorated attempts to criminalise us have
not diminished in any way our determination to pursue and
achieve our republican objectives.

Irish unity and independence provides the best context for
the people of this island to live together in harmony. The
primary responsibility now rests with the two governments.
They must demonstrate their commitment to a lasting peace.
Pandering to the demands of those who are opposed to
change is not the way forward.

This rhetoric of heroes was wearing thin on an increasingly
sceptical and cynical world. The pressure for an end to the war
and decommissioning was growing daily, even as the McCartney
family continued to see first-hand the unchecked intimidation of
witnesses to prevent them telling their stories in court. Even
worse was the fact that the family members themselves were
being targeted by Robert's killers.

At the height of their campaign for justice, Martin
McGuinness warned them to be careful that they were not being
used by others as pawns in a political game. And there's no doubt

political games were being played. The pressure on Sinn Féin and the IRA to fulfil the decommissioning promise had gathered pace, and during the summer of 2005 the Provisionals had another statement to make.

This statement, issued on 28 July, heralded a significant development in the search for lasting peace:

> The leadership of Óglaigh na hÉireann has formally ordered an end to the armed campaign. This will take effect from 4pm [1600 BST] this afternoon [Thursday 28 July 2005]. All IRA units have been ordered to dump arms.
>
> All Volunteers have been instructed to assist the development of purely political and democratic programmes through exclusively peaceful means. Volunteers must not engage in any other activities whatsoever. The IRA leadership has also authorised our representative to engage with the IICD [Independent International Commission on Decommissioning] to complete the process to verifiably put its arms beyond use in a way which will further enhance public confidence and to conclude this as quickly as possible.
>
> We have invited two independent witnesses, from the Protestant and Catholic churches, to testify to this. The Army Council took these decisions following an unprecedented internal discussion and consultation process with IRA units and Volunteers. We appreciate the honest and forthright way in which the consultation process was carried out and the depth and content of the submissions.
>
> We are proud of the comradely way in which this truly historic discussion was conducted. The outcome of our consultations show very strong support among IRA Volunteers for the Sinn Féin peace strategy. There is also widespread concern about the failure of the two governments and the unionists to fully engage in the peace process. This has created real difficulties. The overwhelming majority of people in Ireland fully support this process.
>
> They and friends of Irish unity throughout the world want to see the full implementation of the Good Friday Agreement.

Notwithstanding these difficulties our decisions have been taken to advance our republican and democratic objectives, including our goal of a united Ireland. We believe there is now an alternative way to achieve this and to end British rule in our country. It is the responsibility of all Volunteers to show leadership, determination and courage.

We are very mindful of the sacrifices of our patriot dead, those who went to jail, Volunteers, their families and the wider republican base. We reiterate our view that the armed struggle was entirely legitimate. We are conscious that many people suffered in the conflict. There is a compelling imperative on all sides to build a just and lasting peace. The issue of the defence of nationalist and republican communities has been raised with us.

There is a responsibility on society to ensure that there is no re-occurrence of the pogroms of 1969 and the early 1970s. There is also a universal responsibility to tackle sectarianism in all its forms. The IRA is fully committed to the goals of Irish unity and independence and to building the Republic outlined in the 1916 Proclamation.

We call for maximum unity and effort by Irish republicans everywhere. We are confident that by working together Irish republicans can achieve our objectives. Every Volunteer is aware of the import of the decisions we have taken and all Óglaigh are compelled to fully comply with these orders. There is now an unprecedented opportunity to utilise the considerable energy and goodwill which there is for the peace process.

This comprehensive series of unparalleled initiatives is our contribution to this and to the continued endeavours to bring about independence and unity for the people of Ireland.

At last the final act of decommissioning appeared to be close. Eleven years after the first ceasefires were called, the IRA was on the verge of an historic act.

Confirmation of the final act of decommissioning would come in September with all the predictable rows over whether or not it was done properly and in a fashion acceptable to the unionists.

But there was still evidence of criminal activity by IRA members in spite of the call to cease all operations.

A close friend of Robert McCartney said police have warned him he is under threat from certain individuals in the IRA for testifying about republicans. Jeff Commander, thirty-four, received information about the threat after being attacked and injured in September by up to eight men with iron bars and sewer rods in east Belfast. Two men charged with grievous bodily harm with intent have been remanded in custody. Threats were also made against the man who survived the attack in Magennis's bar, Brendan Devine.

A *Sunday World* journalist, John Cassidy, was also visited by police to inform him there was a threat from members of the IRA.

And the McCartney family—one by one—moved away from the Short Strand area. The intimidation and attacks on their homes became too much to bear.

Paula McCartney said in September that her two teenage sons were beaten recently by family members of a high-ranking IRA officer who they believe was involved in Robert McCartney's killing. This attack followed a few days after the assault on Jeff Commander.

Then there were protests set up outside their homes. Robert McCartney's partner Bridgeen Hagans had crowds of people, mostly women, demonstrating outside her home almost every night demanding she leave the area.

'They want to intimidate us, they want us to keep quiet,' Paula McCartney told an American newspaper reporter who noted that her Short Strand home was decorated with photos of well-wishers including US Senators Edward M. Kennedy, Christopher J. Dodd and Hillary Rodham Clinton.

Paula explained that Commander's attackers used the recent riots in Belfast's Protestant communities as an opportunity to take revenge on McCartney's family while police and public attention were focused elsewhere.

At the time, Mitchell B. Reiss, President Bush's Special Envoy to Northern Ireland, described the situation as 'disgraceful'. He went on to say: 'We deplore the recent violence and intimidation against the McCartney family, Bridgeen and their friends. It is unacceptable and should stop immediately.'

But it did not stop. The IRA might have disarmed and ordered its volunteers to cease all activities, but it did nothing to stop the intimidation and threats by its members in Short Strand.

Paula McCartney's husband Jim Arnold told the *Washington Post* that individual IRA members still act as if they can do anything they want. He described their behaviour as an absolute disgrace and added: 'They are dinosaurs. They live on the back of the IRA, but the IRA are finished, and they cannot grasp it. They won't move on. They're trying to tell our family: Shut up or this is going to happen again. The McCartney family opened a lot of eyes in Belfast.'

In October, Paula McCartney packed her belongings and moved out of the Short Strand—the last member of the family to leave. She said: 'I can't live in a community where it is perfectly acceptable to murder an innocent man and still walk around freely.'

The brave actions of the McCartney family were recognised by the organisers of the Women of the Year event in London in November. Two of Robert McCartney's sisters—Claire and Catherine—were due to attend the presentation at the Guildhall but decided on a point of principle they could not make the trip.

The reason? Former British Prime Minister Margaret Thatcher was also due to receive an award and as republicans the sisters could not countenance accepting the award in her presence.

A statement from the family spelt it out: 'Our campaign is one of justice and as an Irish republican family we feel that we cannot share the same platform as a former Prime Minister who inflicted injuries on our country.'

The IRA thugs responsible for the murder of Robert McCartney and their ongoing cover-up campaign of threat and intimidation could maybe learn something about republican values from this statement.

The police, meanwhile, have continued working towards a

trial. Terence 'Jock' Davison has been charged with Robert McCartney's murder. Davison's friend James McCormick has been charged with the attempted murder of Brendan Devine.

Another leading republican, Gerard 'Jock' Davison—nephew of Terence—publicly denied having given the order to murder Robert McCartney.

At the time of the first court appearance, Paula McCartney said she felt 'nauseated' to see the two accused in the dock, and she repeated that the family expected more criminal charges to be brought against as many as thirteen others who she says were involved in the attack and its attempted cover-up.

'It has to be remembered,' she told reporters, 'that there were a lot more people involved in Robert's murder, and we won't be happy until all those people who were involved are brought to account.'

So as 2005 came to a close, the McCartneys and Bridgeen Hagans prepared for Christmas in their new homes. Sinn Féin and the IRA meanwhile were hoping the year would come to an end as quickly as possible. But 2005 was not finished with the republican movement just yet. As Christmas approached there was another serious setback.

It was the classic good news, bad news scenario.

First the good news came in the form of a decision by the Director of Public Prosecutions not to proceed with the case against three republicans at the centre of the IRA spy ring allegations at Stormont. The three accused returned to Stormont to pose with Sinn Féin leaders. Sinn Féin made the point that the three men had been vindicated.

Unionists argued that the DPP said only that it was not in the public interest to proceed with the case and they demanded an explanation because they knew that as a result of documents and computer discs seized during the police searches of Sinn Féin offices at Stormont, hundreds of people had to be informed that their security had been breached.

But then came the bad news for Sinn Féin. One of the three men, Denis Donaldson, was unmasked as a spy for MI5 and Special Branch. Sinn Féin leader Gerry Adams broke the news to astounded journalists that Donaldson had revealed his secret twenty-year life as a spy when quizzed by party members. Donaldson himself then appeared before television cameras to read a prepared statement in which he confirmed that he had been working for both MI5 and Special Branch. He used the opportunity to criticise Special Branch over the 'spy ring' allegations that had brought about the collapse of the power-sharing Executive, claiming that the investigation had been a sham aimed at politically damaging the peace process.

The pressure cooker year for Sinn Féin had begun with the biggest bank robbery in British history, which was attributed to the IRA, and continued throughout the rest of the year with the fallout from the murder of Robert McCartney. The Colombia Three even turned up in the Republic and presented themselves at Garda stations.

And somewhere in the middle of this torrid twelve months, the IRA decommissioned its weapons.

Meanwhile, if the British and Irish governments were to be believed, members of the newly 'armless' IRA were busying themselves trying to launder £26m of the Northern Bank's money.

06 | WASHING YOUR DIRTY MONEY IN PUBLIC

'*The IRA has an extremely sophisticated money gathering operation and is very capable of getting into profit through a whole range of business operations—pubs owned by former Army Council members, for example, buying up pockets of land and developing it for housing. The money gives the Provos great power. And they have been manipulating the system down south for years.*'—SENIOR MEMBER OF GARDAÍ

Money knows no political boundaries. Cash is cash. It's not republican cash; it's not loyalist cash and it's not ODC cash. ODC? Ordinary decent criminal.

While loyalists, republicans and ordinary decent criminals share a love of cash, the paramilitaries would have you believe that's where the similarities end.

What I am trying to say is that throughout the three decades of conflict, the loyalist and republican paramilitaries would have you believe they were 'soldiers' fighting a just war to protect God and Ulster or to force a united Ireland through British withdrawal from the occupied six counties. 'They' were political. Definitely not 'criminal'. 'They' looked down their noses at the criminals—or quite frequently, down the barrel of a gun aimed at kneecaps or elbow joints of an 'anti-social' offender.

But guess what? This stance of principled intolerance towards criminals conveniently overlooks the fact that it is crime that funds the gunmen and bombers. They conveniently overlook the fact that their cash comes from crime. Income from armed robberies, kidnappings, drugs, extortion, building scams, smuggling fuel and cigarettes has been essential in financing more than thirty years of murder and mayhem. It's what has funded terrorist arsenals.

But in order to use their stolen cash, the men of principle need the help of ordinary decent criminals. They need people who can help them clean up their cash—in other words, launder it through whatever system is necessary to get the money moving around the world or into legitimate bank accounts where it can more easily be accounted for and used. For when it comes to laundering money, odcs are an essential ingredient. There's no moral high ground.

Money laundering is the term used to describe how money gained through criminal activity is eventually brought back from the black economy into the regular economy that we use. It is often a difficult process to unravel. But during the long years of the conflict the paramilitaries fine-tuned their skills at hiding the proceeds of their criminal enterprises. In order to survive financially they have been inventive and enterprising in the many and various ways they clean their cash. The police always seem to be playing catch-up.

As Chief Inspector Sam Sittlington—an experienced financial investigation officer with the Police Service of Northern Ireland —told me, tougher money laundering legislation is vital:

Criminals are always trying to keep ahead of law enforcement. We're always playing catch-up. They will always try new methods.

But the new legislation that has been brought in, the Proceeds of Crime Act, the use of ara (Assets Recovery Agency) as well, where we don't have to have a criminal conviction—all that assists us.

The anti-money laundering regulations where banks have to disclose to the National Criminal Intelligence Service, where solicitors and accountants have to disclose; all that is fairly new within this past couple of years. So anti-money laundering regulation helps us and we can only learn from new cases and new investigations how criminals are trying to manoeuvre money.

They do need the help of solicitors and accountants, and they need to use the banking system to move money. So all of that is important and if we maintain the regulations and obligations placed on us, that'll help us. But everybody has to co-operate. Everybody has to be involved and singing from the same hymn sheet and visibly trying to make it harder for the criminal to move his money.

Sittlington speaks with authority and an intimate knowledge of the many and nefarious ways criminals have found to launder their cash. In the summer of 2005 at Belfast Crown Court he witnessed the conclusion of a six-year investigation into a money laundering operation that took him half-way around the world and involved police and customs all over Europe, the Middle East and even the Far East.

The case centred on a small bureau de change along the main Belfast-Dublin road at Dromad, south of Newry and close to Dundalk.

Cash exchanges sprang up in border areas after the Irish government opted out of sterling in March 1979 to set up the Irish pound, better known as the punt. This particular bureau was not opened until the early nineties.

Sam Sittlington's interest in Dromad began with disclosures from banks in the south Armagh area of suspicious activities involving a local businessman. It was 1999. Apparently a man running a small soft drinks business was purchasing bank drafts for large amounts of cash.

He recalled his involvement when we talked after his six-year investigation ended in successful prosecutions in the spring of 2005:

A bank made a disclosure to us in relation to a company based here in the border area, in Forkhill. The disclosure was that this guy has a soft drinks company and he appears to be purchasing drafts for over £200,000 a time and is sending them to foreign jurisdictions.

Following up leads and the necessary paper trail, Sittlington was soon drawn to the cash exchange at Dromad.

In truth, while this lead was to be a major breakthrough in terms of the money laundering taking place at the Dromad bureau de change, Sittlington had already been looking closely at the activities there in conjunction with the Gardaí south of the border.

And what they were about to find was a major criminal enterprise—a money laundry with hundreds of millions of pounds in turnover . . . and all this activity taking place next door to the other tenants of the building—the Gardaí.

The amounts of cash flowing through the Dromad money exchange were absolutely staggering, according to Sittlington:

> When we counted the monies up over a two and a half year period, there was a quarter of a billion turnover within the bureau. That was as much as the bureau in the Central Bank of Ireland would do in six months.

What the police internationally learned from this long and complex investigation perfectly illustrates how advanced criminals have become at laundering their cash and keeping it away from the prying eyes of the authorities. So it's worthwhile taking a closer look at the money laundering expertise on offer at Dromad.

This journey of discovery had its origins in 1997 following the bizarre death of a major drug trafficker in Drogheda. The body of Paddy Farrell, from the Newry area, was found in the bedroom of a house where he was secretly meeting his mistress for a night of passion. He was found shot to death—the body of his young lover was found beside him. It's thought that she first murdered him and then turned the gun on herself.

But it is not a universally accepted explanation. The *Sunday World*'s Hugh Jordan, for one, is not entirely convinced:

He met a dreadful death. He maintained a double life. He was married and had a family but he had a girlfriend—of the same name funnily enough, Lorraine Farrell—and the two of them were found in what could only be described as bizarre circumstances, where a hood was put over Farrell's head and then it is alleged that Lorraine Farrell shot him as they were engaged in some sort of sexual activity, and then shot herself.

But the circumstances of the death have not been conclusively revealed. There is still a question mark over if this was actually what happened or was it made to look like that. There have been suggestions that some organisation abducted both of them and, having killed them, made it look as though they had taken their own life, or that she had taken first of all his life and then her own, but there was no simple and safe conclusion to all of that.

A major criminal like Paddy Farrell undoubtedly had enemies. You don't climb the criminal ladder without losing friends. And you don't operate any criminal activity along the border without reaching some kind of understanding with the IRA. The IRA commander in the border area levied a 'drug tax' on Farrell of around £5,000 a month.

Paddy Farrell had risen from relative obscurity to become a major criminal. He was a lorry driver from the Newry area and, like many other lorry drivers along the border, he quickly learned that there were more ways to make money than just driving a lorry.

Farrell started off by bringing parts of vehicles into the country and also established a network for selling ringer vehicles —a business operation that first brought him to the attention of the police.

Then, according to Hugh Jordan, he found another lucrative activity:

Later on he developed links particularly in the drug business and he had a couple of major drug dealers who later became very well known working for him. One was a man called

Paddy Doyle who is currently in jail on serious drugs convictions in Belgium, and the more famous Brendan Speedy Fagan who was later murdered by the IRA for being a major, major drug dealer.

Farrell quickly established his credentials as a serious player in the drugs business. He set up importation routes to bring drugs into the country. He became more and more wealthy—and powerful. At the time of Farrell's sudden demise, Felix McKenna was a senior officer involved with the Garda fraud unit:

> Paddy Farrell was shot dead in Drogheda in September of 1997 and subsequent to his death, I—as then chief of the fraud squad—and jointly along with the Criminal Assets Bureau, began a process of examining his assets in Ireland and elsewhere throughout the world.
>
> We were in the position to identify that Paddy Farrell was using the bureau [at Dromad] more or less as an unlicensed bank and a facilitator for himself for a period of about two and a half years prior to his death. He was using it through an alias that he had at the bureau, as a regular customer. He used to call and make deposits on a monthly basis. He was very regular in respect of his deposits, and the records showed that he deposited the exact amount every month.

So promising was the Farrell asset trail that the Gardaí set up a major surveillance operation on the Dromad bureau that lasted for two years. And during that time the scope of the investigation had to be widened, as McKenna recalled:

> In that two-year period, a number of international meetings took place between agencies—that is, the financial investigation unit of the RUC, financial profilings of customs and excise in the North of Ireland and England.
>
> We liaised with the Drug Enforcement Agency and the FBI in America and a number of agencies in London. And between ourselves and Irish customs, we were—shall we say

—gathering intelligence on the Farrell asset portfolio in England and America. We were also gathering intelligence on the activities of the money flows that were being generated from this unlicensed institution.

Felix McKenna said there was more business in this institution than there would've been in one of the High Street banks in Dundalk.

According to Sittlington, the Dromad bureau was set up in the early 1990s by Farrell and the family of Kieran Byrne—the man responsible for running it. Until Farrell's death the bureau had not been under the kind of close police and customs scrutiny it was now experiencing.

After Farrell's death in 1997, the reality of the Dromad bureau soon became apparent. It was set up by a criminal to be run as an unlicensed bank for criminals and its enormous turnover of £2,500m during the two years it was under surveillance was entirely for the benefit of those who were using it for criminal purposes.

In terms of money laundering, Dromad was an industrial-strength washing machine.

The more the police delved, the more intrigued they became, and the intensity of the international meetings increased. Felix McKenna explained it:

> During all of those meetings, the agencies shared intelligence and information. We attempted to profile what was going on at the border bureau and how it was being used, particularly by a variety of criminals.
>
> And we also discovered during that period of time, unbeknown to ourselves, that there was a surveillance operation being conducted in Dublin by the Garda National Drugs Unit into a person who was suspected of being the bagman for drug traffickers based in Dublin and also in Manchester.
>
> As a result of that surveillance, we learned subsequently that that bagman visited Dromad on a number of occasions

with a plastic bag of Irish currency. He was facilitated with the exchange; he was handed back sterling—usually in sums of about £100,000 at a time. His MO then was that he would transport the sterling to Manchester by airplane, rather than sending it through a licensed bank.

For the two years they secretly spied on the bureau—and remember a police station was located next door in the other half of the building which was rented by the Gardaí from the owners of the bureau—they witnessed the comings and goings of all sorts of criminals.

According to Sittlington:

> The bureau was acting as an illegal bank. They had about 100-150 account holders. The account holders would bring in cash. They actually had £1m in their safe and the bureau then would transfer that money anywhere in the world for the account holders.
>
> All the account holders within the bank were smugglers—oil, fuel, cigarettes, milk quotas . . . the whole shebang—drug traffickers. It was a facility there on the border for all local criminals.

The police also identified that the bureau itself was using banks on both sides of border. As McKenna put it: 'The case grew in momentum over the next two years. So it was time to do a—as we call it—a "knock", that is a joint search operation in both the North and the South of Ireland and also a number of searches in England.'

The date chosen for 'Operation Factual' in the South and 'Operation Beaumont' in the North was 18 October 1999. Twenty-five premises were targeted.

More than 300 police and customs officers were involved in the planned searches. Up to now they had been dependent on the results of their surveillance and intelligence reports. Now they were going to finally have access to the bureau and see inside the safes at the bureau and other safes at the homes and businesses of the Byrne family. In the bureau alone they recovered over £1m in cash. Bank accounts were frozen with hundreds of thousands of pounds in them.

But the most important breakthrough of all happened at the home of a member of the Byrne family, as McKenna recalled:

> The operation commenced early in the morning and during the search operation a large amount of cash was found in a variety of small safes that were in Dromad itself or in the parent's houses, so all of that cash was seized. But the real bonus was that we found all of the records or supposedly records of Dromad; their banking records. We found them in the boot of the car parked outside one of the houses that we searched. They had been removed from the office a number of days before we had done the search, so luckily enough we search everything in these operations.
>
> And all the cheque stubs and the daily record sheets etc. were in the boot of the car. So as a result of finding all of that material and particularly the ledgers that were used, we were then able to build a profile of the amounts of money that were being siphoned through Dromad and the facilities that the owner was providing for large amounts of people that are involved in the criminal world along the border.

Close inspection of the books at Dromad told police tales that they found hard to believe: tales of drugs and of worldwide smuggling . . . of murder . . . and of money laundering on a gigantic scale.

They discovered that the man who ran the bureau, Kieran Byrne, allowed all the account holders to use false names. This, of course, included Paddy Farrell, who apparently had several of them. False names also concealed the identities of terrorist customers.

McKenna told me:

> From the intelligence and the information available to us, we have investigated a number of individuals that are based

along the border, both on the Southern side and the Northern side. Since those years, a number of the customers that we have identified in Dromad . . . that were using Dromad . . . have subversive links. There were also a number of customers in Dromad ledgers that we are unable to identify.

The reason we have been unable to identify them is that the staff of the bureau were unable to co-operate with us and unable to identify how these people were recorded in their books. Because you must bear in mind that the record system that was run in Dromad, people were identified by their initials or they had no names written in the account books. So it took some time to actually identify individuals, and you gathered that by intelligence and information.

In Dromad, the ledgers recorded customer transactions in 'UP' columns for deposits and 'DOWN' columns for withdrawals. And to illustrate just how casual the system was, the police found a number of transactions for substantial sums of money that were simply attributed to 'Joe's Mate'.

It is little wonder that the Central Bank of Ireland rejected an application from the Dromad bureau for a license to run as a bank!

The Gardaí prosecuted Kieran Byrne for money laundering and running an illegal bank. He was sentenced to five years imprisonment with the final year suspended.

Parallel to that, the Gardaí's Criminal Assets Bureau examined Byrne's asset portfolio. They discovered he had property and bank accounts in Ireland, the Isle of Man and a number of other jurisdictions including Spain. Byrne's assets were frozen and he was obliged to pay €3.5m to the revenue authorities in settlement.

Meanwhile, Sam Sittlington's work was only beginning with the raids conducted in 1999. By this stage he had identified the Forkhill soft drinks businessman who had been reported by the banks to be buying large bank drafts for distribution all over the world. His name was Kenneth Mackin.

The bank drafts led to Holland. And this in turn would lead law enforcement agencies into the heart of a major laundering operation . . .

In Rotterdam, the Dutch customs authorities were engaged in a number of operations to break up gangs of cigarette smugglers. One of the gangs included a number of Irishmen, and two in particular were in their sights—Kieran Smyth from the Dundalk area and Martin Daly from Northern Ireland. A surveillance operation had begun.

Under the auspices of the European Union's anti-fraud office in Brussels, the Dutch had been going to the meetings in Ireland organised by the Gardaí and the PSNI. They were fully aware of what was going on during the two-year surveillance operation at Dromad.

What the Dutch were interested in resolving was the mystery of how the smuggled cigarettes were being paid for. They knew the identities of the Dutch criminals who were working with the Irish on enormous shipments of contraband cigarettes. Now they were about to find out how the money was passed on to the Dutch criminals.

Phone taps revealed that a consignment of smuggled cigarettes was on its way from Italy via a warehouse in Belgium to Rotterdam. Tipped off by Dutch customs, Belgian customs officers took charge. Dutch undercover customs investigator Rob van Zijp told me what happened: 'They entered the warehouse and there they found Irish people with their hands on cigarettes, who were smuggling from Italy. The Belgian authorities seized more than twenty-one million cigarettes at the time.'

Kieran Smyth was one of those caught in the warehouse. But in order to preserve the Dutch operation, the Belgians agreed to release Smyth after a period of questioning in detention. Released from prison, Smyth was soon back in business in Holland—his every move monitored as the authorities there tried to intercept more illegal cargo—this time in Rotterdam itself.

As a result, the Dutch were able to observe Smyth, his Irish friend Martin Daly, and their gang moving vast quantities of cigarettes. A company called Universal in Rotterdam was involved.

According to Rob van Zijp, three containers of cigarettes were found in Universal's warehouse. Twenty-one million cigarettes were hidden in what was supposed to be a cargo of Chinese porcelain. Telephone taps made it clear that the cigarettes were destined for a location near the Irish border.

But even better, Universal proved to be a major breakthrough. During questioning, staff there revealed details of another large shipment. This time it was eighteen containers with 160 million contraband cigarettes coming from Malta, through Italy to Rotterdam.

The Dutch seized the cargo. But they still had no idea how the Irish buyers actually paid for the cigarettes. And then a clue from one of their wiretaps . . . a clue linked the contraband directly to Dromad. A member of the Dutch gang was asking another Dutchman about how the payment would be made. When he mentioned the name Kieran, the other man gave him a telephone number for what he referred to as 'the bank'. The other man knew then what he meant and hung up.

Checks linked the telephone number to the Dromad bureau. Finally, with the help of the police north and south of the border, the Dutch would find out how the Irish smugglers Kieran Smyth and Martin Daly paid for the cigarette shipments to Ireland.

Felix McKenna was able to tell them that Kieran Smyth was the owner of a road transport company and that he had come to the attention of the Garda Drug Squad some time earlier when a shipment of drugs and weapons was intercepted near the Irish border at a town called Castleblayney.

Smyth's company was on its knees financially . . . but you wouldn't think it if you looked at the Dromad accounts. Sam Sittlington discovered that he had moved a substantial amount of money from the bureau to various countries—in excess of £14m.

To arrive at that conclusion, the police first had to decipher the coded list of Dromad account holders; aware, of course, that most used false names. Eventually, the police trawl through the list of bureau regulars came upon the name James Paul.

Sam Sittlington explained the significance:

When we looked at the James Paul account we saw £14m

being moved out of the bureau. We looked at that closely and
we were able to connect that to Kieran Smyth and Martin
Daly. Then we looked closely at them and it simply is their
middle names. They were using a false name and it was the
middle names of both of them as the account holder.

The Dutch eventually tracked Daly to Turkey and had him
arrested. A Turkish court extradited him to Rotterdam where he
was convicted along with six Dutchmen. He got a light prison
sentence.

However, Kieran Smyth had managed to flee Holland for what
he thought was the safety of home in Ireland. But as the Dutch
pursued him with a warrant, he was kidnapped from his home
near Dundalk. Smyth was held for two weeks before being shot
dead. His body was dumped on a farm near Ashbourne on the
outskirts of Dublin. His death bore all the hallmarks of an IRA
assassination and that was one line of inquiry being followed by
the Gardaí. They were also of the opinion that Smyth had been
killed over a disagreement with the Provisionals over his
smuggling scams. No one has ever been brought before the courts
for the murder.

The Dromad records were invaluable in helping Sam
Sittlington solve the mystery transactions involving the soft
drinks businessman, Kenneth Mackin, while at the same time
assisting the Dutch discover the method of payment for the
cigarettes. Kieran Smyth and Martin Daly could not have sent
£14m around the world to pay for their contraband cigarettes
without the co-operation of Kieran Byrne, the Dromad owner.
And—in turn—Byrne could not have helped Smyth and Daly
without the co-operation of Kenneth Mackin and his brother
Raymond.

Here's how it worked. It was a classic money-laundering
operation. Kieran Smyth would tell Kieran Byrne that he needed
to get a bank draft for £250,000, for example. Byrne would
contact the Mackin brothers. He would tell Kenneth Mackin that
he needed to raise £250,000 and he would ask: 'How many
containers of Coca-Cola do you need to for that amount?'

This reference to Coca-Cola relates to the soft drinks business the Mackins had set up. Of course, it was just a sham—a cover for their criminal activity.

The Mackins set up two companies—Kemac north of the border and Kepal south of the border. Kemac wanted to sell Coca-Cola to Kepal in the South . . . in other words Kenneth Mackin was selling Coke to himself.

But they needed a 'Mr Clean' to be involved in these bogus transactions so that it would look to any casual outside observer—such as a police officer or customs inspector—like there was legitimate business being done.

So Mackin approached a legitimate company in England—Goodness Foods Ltd—to buy Coca-Cola from his company Kemac north of the border and then sell it on to Kepal south of the border.

But rather than send all that Coca-Cola from Kemac in Northern Ireland to Goodness Foods in England and leave Goodness Foods the logistical problem of delivering the consignment of Coca-Cola to Kepal in the Republic of Ireland, Kenneth Mackin told Goodness Foods that he would organise the transport of the Coca-Cola for them. He would send it on the thirty-mile journey himself.

According to Sam Sittlington, the use of Goodness Foods Ltd as a 'broker' in such a business arrangement is not uncommon. But, of course, the reality in this example is that there was no Coca-Cola to transport—the only thing to move were false invoices and a VAT fraud.

The Coca-Cola scam is linked directly to the cigarette smuggling and the Dromad money laundering operations—and it is now used as an exercise to train detectives in money laundering techniques.

This is how Det. Insp. Sittlington explained it:

So one of the account holders was Mr Smyth. He was a tobacco smuggler and he wanted money sent out to Hong Kong. He would ring the bureau and say, 'I need £215k sent to Hong Kong.' Mr Bureau would ring Mr Mackin and say to Mr

Mackin: 'We need to make up £215k here: how many loads of Coca-Cola would that take?' And he would say it takes fifteen loads. So he rings up Goodness Foods in England and says: 'Buy fifteen loads of Coca-Cola from me.' And then he sells it back to Kepal. The paper shift starts; the money starts to move and the money ends up in Mr Mackin's account and he goes to the bank and buys a bankers' draft for £215k and gives that to Kieran Byrne to send that off to Hong Kong.

Kieran Smyth's money—lodged in the bureau in the James Paul account—would remain there. But once he wanted to raise a bank draft, the bureau would instruct one of the banks in the area where it had accounts to electronically transfer funds to Goodness Food in England. This represented the payment to Goodness Foods from Kepal, the Mackin company in the South. Once Kepal paid Goodness Foods, the English company would then deduct their percentage and forward the remainder to Kemac in the North. This gave Kenneth Mackin the funds to purchase a bank draft for the £215,000 the bureau boss Kieran Byrne needed to help Kieran Smyth send cash abroad for smuggled cigarettes.

The Mackins' fantasy Coke trail was producing more sales than the drink manufacturers needed for the whole of Ireland. To make this scam sing in perfect harmony, someone had to transport all this Coke . . . up to fifteen containers a day. Enter James Convery, a Newry road haulier. His role in all this make-believe was to agree to generate paperwork to show he was delivering Coca-Cola from Kemac in the North to Kepal south of the border.

Mind you, at fifteen containers a day both he and Coca-Cola might have wished it *was* the real thing. The only genuine part of the Coke scam was the money transferred to Goodness Foods almost every day for two years—it added a staggering £17m to their turnover—*their* share of that was £600,000.

Kenneth Mackin's only profit from this was on the VAT fraud. But it was a good little earner for him . . . and one he wanted to protect. When police searched his home they found his escape pack ... a case packed with £50,000 in cash, his passport and bank cards.

The essential ingredients in the money laundering exercise described above are that the Mackins had two shell companies that neither produced nor sold any product; they fooled a legitimate company into taking part in their scam and they had the services of an illegal bank to keep them away for the most part from the high street banks. Along the way they also produced 'fake' invoices to cover the buying and selling of the non-existent Coca-Cola and the costs of transporting it. Following this paper trail is difficult and troublesome for the authorities as it creates a paper trail equivalent to a smoke screen.

Felix McKenna summed it up:

> At the time, as a result of the figures that we were looking at for the previous two years, when we did the search operation in 1999 it brought us to realise that there is a huge cash culture in this part of the world and that people require cash to do business. And the bureau itself was there as a vehicle to operate, shall we say, totally unlicensed, totally unpoliced and they were operating in a poor and black economy and this was again the illegal bank that facilitated people who wanted to avoid all types of systems.
>
> Now I'm talking about criminals who would be involved in a variety of activities, particularly smuggling of cigarettes and all, this is a vehicle that they were using to move their money around in. On the international side of things, it also identified the activities and the amount of monies available to them. So the figures that we actually identified that had been moved through this institution were astronomical in comparison to, shall we say, main street banks. There was more business in this institution than there would've been in one of the high street banks in Dundalk.

Of course, after the police operations closed Dromad in 1999, none of the bureau regulars came forward to the Gardaí to claim the cash deposits seized during the searches. It meant the fight against crime in the Republic benefited to the tune of over £1m.

Naturally, the Gardaí and the PSNI continued their efforts to try to identify the owners of the seized cash, with limited success. But they did uncover links to paramilitary groups like the IRA, as Felix McKenna told me:

> From the intelligence and the information available to us, we have investigated a number of individuals that are based along the border, both on the Southern side and the Northern side. Since those years, a number of the customers that we have identified in Dromad, that were using Dromad, have subversive links.

Sam Sittlington said it would have been impossible for the Dromad bureau to operate in the border area without paramilitary approval:

> With substantial amounts of money in the border area, persons involved in fuel and cigarette smuggling and drug trafficking and money laundering—I've always said that no one in the border area could operate that type of business without some sort of authority or approval from the paramilitaries in that area.

In other words, the IRA used the bureau. Certainly, IRA chief of staff Thomas 'Slab' Murphy had occasion to stash cash there. For a start, there was the £5,000 monthly payment from Paddy Farrell before his death in 1997. No doubt those who took over running Farrell's drug empire would be expected to maintain the payments.

—

But even as the Gardaí were watching the bureau and preparing for the searches in the autumn of 1999, there were a number of money transactions that caught the eye of police officers in Florida.

The Americans were investigating a gunrunning operation that involved the IRA. This would eventually lead the FBI back to the infamous Dromad bureau de change.

A number of illegally held handguns from the US had been discovered in Ireland and the United Kingdom. Scotland Yard detectives contacted the FBI to try to pin down the origins of the weapons in the United States.

The guns had been sent to Ireland and the UK through the postal service from various post offices in Florida. Scotland Yard provided serial numbers for the weapons seized so far and when the FBI put the numbers of those weapons into the system, they discovered that the purchase of these particular guns was under investigation by an agent in the Fort Lauderdale office of the ATF (Alcohol, Tobacco & Firearms).

The ATF had been alerted by the multiple gun purchases of an Irish-American citizen, Siobhan Brown. All multiple gun purchases must be reported to the ATF by the dealer who sells them. The ATF agent on this case, Regina Lombardo, noticed that a false address had been given by the buyer.

Florida is a magnet for gunrunners because of its lax gun laws. It's as easy to buy a gun as it is to buy a car. As a result, Florida is a major source of weapons procurement for crime and terrorist syndicates.

I discovered just how easy it is to buy heavy weaponry even for non-American citizens as long as residency can be proved when I spoke to Al Richards who owns a gun shop in Fort Lauderdale. He explained the rules: 'If you are a citizen of the United States and a resident of this state, then you could buy one of these guns. You would have a seven day waiting period . . . once you pass the background check you go out the door with it. If they lived here ninety days they can qualify.'

But not all gun dealers follow procedures. The middle-class suburban area of Boynton Beach, Fort Lauderdale, is the unlikely trading centre for Big Shot Firearms. Gun dealer Edward Bluestein operates quietly from home. At 9 p.m. on 29 April 1999, 34-year-old Cork-born Siobhan Brown, now an American citizen, drove up to the Bluestein household to collect five handguns ordered four days earlier at a gun show in Fort Lauderdale.

Later that evening, Brown's 42-year-old boyfriend joined her. Belfast-born Anthony Smyth had lived in America for the past eleven years. According to the ATF, the couple told Edward Bluestein they wanted to buy as many guns as he could supply for 'a cause they were devoted to'. They would fax him a list.

The handwritten list included numerous high-powered weapons and numerous concealable weapons:

> 'any small concealable .25 and up'
> 'anything silenced .25 and up'
> 'any full auto sub machine guns...the smaller the better'
> 'Heckler & Koch MP5K Auto (in briefcase if possible)'

Brown's weapon purchases were put on the ATF's multiple purchase database at its field office at the Federal Building in Fort Lauderdale. Agent Lombardo discovered that the address given by Brown on an ATF purchase form (4473) was false. Her job was to track down Siobhan Brown. But that was easier said than done.

When the ATF took up the trail of Siobhan Brown their first port of call was a mailbox rental service in Fort Lauderdale, an address she often gave on official documents. They discovered that she had another mailbox rental in a different part of the city.

They say they also established that Siobhan Brown used two other names, had two social security numbers and two Florida driving licences. Later in court, the US prosecutor said she lived her life without any physical location—describing her lifestyle as 'murky'.

But by putting surveillance on her mailbox facility, the authorities hoped to learn more about Siobhan Brown's lifestyle.

ATF agent Lombardo told me that Siobhan Brown appeared in her photographs to be an older, more conservative woman. But her alias, Mary Brown, was portrayed as a younger person in photographs. She also sometimes used her married name, Mary Siobhan Rapaport, even though estranged from her husband. The checks on Brown began to pay dividends.

A pattern of prolific gun buying by the Irish woman with no address quickly emerged. At the Firearms Plus store Brown was remembered as a very distinctive customer. She had a strong Irish accent and, unusually, did not haggle over prices. Other gun dealers in the Fort Lauderdale area were also able to identify her from driving licence pictures. There was no disputing the fact that Siobhan Brown and Mary Brown purchased weapons.

What quickly became clear to the ATF was that Brown was not acting alone. Dealers informed them that a man accompanied her on her gun buying expeditions. The continuing watch on her mailbox revealed that letters addressed to a Conor Claxton— from Belfast—were being delivered there as well.

Kenny Hale worked in the mailbox rental and he told me about Claxton:

> He would pick it up occasionally and he was a . . . I think he told me he was Conor Claxton the first time. He had an Irish accent. I'd say maybe six weeks before she got arrested they [the ATF] came in and they started asking me some questions and what I could say . . . and then they gave me a subpoena to give all the records and I gave them the forms I had and the information and then they had me make copies of her mail. Just the outside of the envelope, nothing else, 'cause I couldn't open it legally.

Although it was clear from photographs identified by dealers that it wasn't Claxton who had been with Brown when she was buying guns, the ATF discovered that he had shared an apartment with Brown and her boyfriend, Anthony Smyth, at Brown's previous address. The scale and manner of the purchases led Lombardo to send Brown's file to the ATF's international intelligence unit in Washington. She named Claxton, Smyth and Brown, and included the serial numbers of the guns bought. The timing was fortuitous.

As further packages were intercepted by the Irish and British postal services with weapons concealed in video recorders, toys and computers, and as Scotland Yard and the FBI began investigating who was responsible, the ATF file was transmitted through Interpol and immediately attracted a red flag for terrorism. It was a lucky break.

FBI agent Mark Hastbacka explained:

> I'd received some serial numbers from Scotland Yard and was attempting to identify the purchasers of some firearms. Unknown to me at the time, Ms Lombardo was running a parallel investigation on a multiple purchase of firearms by Siobhan Brown, and some of the serial numbers that I was enquiring about that had been recovered over in Scotland Yard were being investigated by the ATF.

FBI traces established that Smyth had also bought twenty-six handguns and six shotguns, informing Edward Bluestein that they would never be seen again in America and that the serial numbers would be removed.

Constant surveillance paid off and unexpectedly introduced a fourth suspect. Agents tailed Claxton from his hotel apartment at Deerfield Beach to another hotel nearby and watched him meet 29-year-old Martin Mullan.

Mullan, from Dunloy in County Antrim, had checked in nine days earlier. He was one of a number of people who signed assent forms for Ballymoney Sinn Féin councillor Martin O'Neill in 1997. The surveillance team watched Mullan and Claxton leave the hotel and load parcels and luggage into their cars.

The two men left in different directions. At this point the FBI tailing Mullan in his Mitsubishi Eclipse lost him at traffic lights. Checks revealed that the vehicle was not registered and bore false number plates.

The authorities decided it was time to close the net. With Smyth, Claxton and Brown in custody, they discovered that Mullan had gone to Philadelphia. He was immediately arrested and extradition warrants were sought to bring him back to Florida.

The arrests and allegations of IRA gunrunning during their ceasefire was yet another threat to the peace process in Ireland.

Siobhan Brown admitted smuggling guns to the IRA from

Florida and was jailed for twenty months by a US court in August 2000. After a five-week trial the other defendants—Anthony Smyth, Martin Mullan and Conor Claxton—were found guilty of buying and illegally shipping weapons from Florida through the US mail service.

They also received jail terms but were cleared of the more serious charge of conspiracy to commit murder and maim in Northern Ireland and providing material support to terrorists.*

In court, the FBI claimed that Claxton admitted involvement with the IRA. The FBI told the court:

> Claxton acknowledged that he was sent by someone higher up in his organisation, the Provisional IRA, whom he would not identify. Claxton stated that the guns he was shipping through the US postal service were not to be used against any children and were only to be used against the British soldiers, the police forces of Northern Ireland, who Claxton referred to as the RUC, and Protestant paramilitaries, all of whom he referred to as being under the control of the Crown.

Naturally, Claxton denied making such comments—just as republicans denied involvement in the gunrunning scam, until the IRA felt compelled to issue this ambiguous statement:

> Following recent media reports of an alleged arms importation operation from the USA, a preliminary investigation has been concluded by Óglaigh na hÉireann. The Army Council has not sanctioned any arms importation operation. Let us emphasise that there have been no breaches of the IRA cessation, which remains intact.

The search of Claxton's room at the Buccaneer Hotel on Deerfield Beach was revealing. The FBI's list of items removed from Claxton's apartment included laser sights and ten handguns —three already packaged for postage. Documents and a document shredder were seized along with credit cards and

---

* Four people were imprisoned in the Irish Republic in 2002 on similar offences.

American bank account details, as well as passports in different names. Gun catalogues, airline tickets and a laptop computer were also removed, along with two pairs of rubber gloves and a black beret . . . and a book on how to change your identity.

It was abundantly clear that the gunrunning gang was exceptionally well-funded. Although Brown had used her own credit cards for some of the transactions, it was immediately apparent to the FBI that Claxton was in charge of the operation. He had two American bank accounts. Funds were paid into his accounts from Ireland.

Tracing back some of those payments led the US and Irish authorities to Dromad. The bureau was at the time under surveillance from 1997 right up to the point of the police searches in October 1999. Cash from the bureau was being taken out to create electronic transfers of funds to Florida for the gunrunning operation.

—

The closure of Dromad damaged the ability of its criminal clientele to operate, but, as Felix McKenna pointed out, it wasn't long before an alternative was found:

> Immediately the criminals set up another institution somewhat forty miles along the border, and that was subsequently closed down as a result of a joint operation and people are before the courts, so I cannot really discuss it. So, they just move location if they need this business to actually conceal their monies and generate bank drafts.

The money laundering operation at Dromad is a good example of what is needed to take dirty money and distribute it around the world or to clean it up for use at home. But there are other alternatives. Cash businesses hold an attraction for the cleansing of dirty money. And all that's required is a businessman running such a business who needs a financial boost for his flagging fortunes.

Felix McKenna explained:

World experts describe money laundering as a three-tier layering process. The criminals generate their huge profits from crime—let it be, for example, a simple thing like an armed robbery, or they have suddenly come into possession of a large amount of cash.

In order for them to cleanse that, they must find some system whereby they layer it into the financial process and some of the methodologies that they have used where a business is down on its luck, they go to the owner and say: 'We want you to launder X amounts of thousands for us, or hundreds of thousands for us.' Or they go into a business that's cash-oriented, for argument's sake a petrol station or public house—they are cash businesses.

They could introduce a lot of their dirty money into their legitimate business and that way, over a long period of time, launder all of their cash. If they want to do it quickly they must find some institution that will take large amounts of monies off them, or shall we say a rogue professional, 'cause there are professional laundry people out there like professional criminals who know the financial system intimately. They know where to lodge the monies where it will not be reported. They use those professional money launderers.

That person will be Mr Clean, he will go through a layering process to disguise the money and it'll eventually come back to the criminal in a clean form. It could come back in the form of a bank draft or a cheque. But there is a complex layering system some of them do, and some of them use a very simple laundering process. For example, they go into a garage, they purchase a motor vehicle for eighty thousand cash, go back one month later and say that they don't like the vehicle and want to trade down. They exchange their eighty thousand vehicle for a twenty thousand car and they are handed back fifty thousand clean money.

So there are a variety of methods the criminals can use to launder their cash. But it is a major phenomemen of major crime bosses throughout the world. I am aware from international investigation and from international intelligence information that some of them specialize in purchasing high value goods like antiques, they can pour large amounts of cash into that business and they can have all of their proceeds of crime hanging on a wall.

But what do you do with £26m? That's a serious amount of cash to launder. The Northern Bank robbers were going to have to be extra inventive to shift that amount of cash.

But remember what money-laundering expert John Horan said earlier about the scale of the challenge with £26m: 'Bizarrely the fact that they had stolen so much money is going to make it very, very difficult to launder.'

So difficult that they might have to consider moving it abroad? Well, yes, according to John Horan:

I think it's inevitable. I think for this amount of money they have a worldwide market where a lot of professional money launderers out there for a percentage of the take will launder the money for them, or will offer to launder the money for them. How successfully is another issue, but bearing in mind the sheer volume of cash taken, that's going to be a very high-risk enterprise for any professional money launderer because the percentage they will want out of it I would imagine will be considerable. But that changes nothing. The profit for the organised crime group that committed the robbery will be massive even if they have to give away fifty or sixty per cent of it.

AUTHOR: And what sort of people might they have to do business with in order to launder this money?

HORAN: There are some—the mafia springs to mind. The American mafia, organised crime groups throughout Europe, throughout the world. There's almost a collection of information and a sharing of information between criminals in the way it is with law enforcement, so the knowledge will be out there to launder the money and a professional money launderer will be trying to make contact with the group to offer their services.

Which leads us to Bulgaria. And Ted Cunningham, a Cork-based financier and moneylender. Undercover Garda Special Branch officers were investigating a republican money laundering and cigarette smuggling operation. Cunningham was associated with cigarette smugglers from along the border—the kind of customers who might have found the Dromad bureau much more convenient but who were compelled to seek help elsewhere —even if it meant looking much further afield and even as far south as Cork.

Special Branch had observed a pair of Bulgarian arms dealers visiting Ireland six months previously. They had a meeting with Cunningham. The undercover police had also witnessed other meetings with a senior IRA man from Northern Ireland. This individual, known to police only by his first name, was extremely cautious about receiving telephone calls. He would often move meetings outdoors to avoid the possibility of the discussion he was having being eavesdropped.

The suspicion was that Cunningham, as a moneylender and financier, may have used business contracts to help republicans launder as much as £7m in recent years. One senior officer told me that during this operation the Gardaí also traced euros that had been exchanged close to the border.

A senior Garda involved in the operation told me:

The closure of Dromad and other cash exchanges like it, meant the thieves were looking to someone who could help them send money to Europe to pay for their smuggled cigarettes and, because of the businesses Cunningham ran, he was able to lodge cash with no suspicions falling on him—no STRs [suspicious transaction reports].

Cunningham was in the business of moneylending and renting properties so he was regularly, in his own business, dealing with cash and his bank was accustomed to that happening. He had an ability to take cash into banks and seek drafts to send to Europe or electronic transfers.

One month after the Northern Bank robbery, as the Garda surveillance operation was continuing on Cunningham, the dramatic events of February 2005 occurred. That's when the Gardaí launched searches at properties in Cork, Louth and Dublin.

It all began at Dublin's Heuston Station around half-past-three on Wednesday 16 February. A passenger who had just stepped off the train from Cork was intercepted by Det. Sgt Rory Corcoran as he was about to get into a Northern Ireland registered four-wheel drive vehicle.

Inside the vehicle the police officer found £54,000 stuffed into a box of Daz washing powder. The man from Cork was thirty-year-old chef Don Bullman—someone who had been under police surveillance for some months.

Two men from Derry who were already in the vehicle were also arrested and questioned before release. They apparently told police they were planning to get the 5 p.m. train to Cork.

Bullman—a father of three and former fundraiser and electoral worker for Sinn Féin—was detained. His arrest set in motion a chain of other Garda operations.

Just a few hours after Bullman's detention in Dublin, two men with Sinn Féin links were arrested at their homes in the Cork area. One of them, Tom Hanlon, a former colleague of Bullman, was arrested at his home in Passage West, Cork. Thirty-seven-year-old Hanlon is a former town councillor and failed Sinn Féin general election candidate.

The other man—George Hegarty from Cork city—also has links to Sinn Féin, and when he was arrested at his Douglas home the police found £60,000 in Northern Bank notes.

Early next morning, 17 February, Gardaí searched Ted Cunningham's business premises. The offices of Chesterton Finance were searched at Ballincollig, outside Cork. Two hours later, at 11 a.m., the Gardaí raided the home of the 56-year-old company director at Farran, about ten miles outside Cork city.

It was here the police made a staggering discovery. Concealed inside a wheelie-bin at Cunningham's home they found £2.3m in sterling bank notes. Cunningham and his business associate Cathy Armstrong were detained for questioning as the police also seized documents.

Initially, police on both sides of the border would not confirm publicly whether or not the notes found in Cunningham's bin were part of the £26.5m Northern Bank robbery. But privately, they did not rule it out.

They followed up every lead they found at Chesterton Finance and at Cunningham's home. The trails picked up from computers and documents set police off on a major paper trail all over Ireland—to accountancy companies and other companies associated with Cunningham's business enterprises.

Later on the same day the Gardaí searched premises in Westmeath, Swords and Offaly as well as three premises in Dundalk in the early evening.

Then, amazingly, a man walked into Anglesea Garda station in Cork city and surrendered £170,000 in cash. The ongoing Garda operation was clearly making some individuals nervous. This man told police he had been given the money by Cunningham.

While Ted Cunningham had been under surveillance by Special Branch for at least nine months prior to all this police activity, now it was time for others to become involved, and the Criminal Assets Bureau was brought into the rapidly expanding investigation.

And, Ireland being Ireland, there was an inevitability that this money laundering investigation would sooner rather than later come face to face with a whiff of political scandal. After all, the Gardaí were on a roll that just kept disgorging shock after shock.

And when it came, it was truly in keeping with everything that had gone before in this stunning story of money laundering, which, at forty-eight hours-of-age, was still in its infancy.

The political face, confronted by Gardaí on his doorstep, belonged to Phil Flynn—a recent adviser to the Taoiseach himself, Bertie Ahern. Here was the political edge of a controversy that has yet to run its full course.

Phil Flynn is a colourful character. Born in Dundalk in 1940, Flynn joined Sinn Féin at the age of fourteen and gave his support to the IRA border campaign of the 1950s. As a consequence of this commitment, he was no stranger to the inside of a Garda barracks.

So it was hardly an unfamiliar experience for Flynn to open his door and find Garda officers standing on his doorstep, this time from the Criminal Assets Bureau (CAB). So on day two of this major police operation, Phil Flynn stepped aside to allow officers to search his Dublin home. They also searched his business premises in the city.

In Dundalk, detectives raided the home and business premises of Flynn's brother James—a mortgage broker.

Like Ted Cunningham, Phil Flynn is a director of Chesterton Finance. And he was observed by undercover Gardaí going to Bulgaria with Cunningham, although he was quick to inform reporters that he met lawyers, bankers, accountants and property developers whilst there. He stressed that he did not meet any arms dealers.

An affirmed and unapologetic republican, Flynn's discomfort over this latest and unwelcome raising of his profile compelled him to resign from a number of high-profile positions in the public and private sectors.

A former vice-president of Sinn Féin and a trade union leader of high repute, Flynn made rapid advancement up the 'corporate' ladder. But as soon as this proverbial hit the fan he resigned from three key positions:
- as chairman of the government committee on decentralisation
- as chairman of Bank of Scotland (Ireland)
- as a director of VHI, the health insurance company

The resignations came within hours of his name being associated with the police actions against Ted Cunningham. Flynn also told reporters that before he agreed to join Cunningham at Chesterton Finance, he had checked the company out and believed it to be above board.

Flynn insisted that Chesterton was 'clean', and said that his trip to Bulgaria was for legitimate business reasons. He added that he had hoped to set up a firm similar to Chesterton and had looked at the possibility of opening a mortgage firm there.

Chesterton made profit out of the misfortune of individuals who had been turned down by mainstream banks and was able to charge higher interests rates—up to 24 per cent in some cases. Flynn's critics argued that this was a grubby business for such a prominent 'establishment' figure as Flynn to become involved with.

When Flynn was first approached by the moneylender Ted Cunningham he got his former banking colleague Denis O'Connell to carry out a company check. He decided to join as a director and pointed Chesterton in the direction of the lucrative and largely cash-based Bulgarian market, where holiday villas can change hands for as little as €40,000.

In an interview with RTÉ television, Flynn said he had no involvement—'good, bad or indifferent'—in money laundering and he rejected any suggestion that he might have been exploited by people he knew in the republican movement.

He also acknowledged that his directorship of the company at the centre of the Garda investigation was perhaps an error of judgement, although he also stated his belief that Chesterton Finance would be cleared of any wrongdoing.

He told the RTÉ reporter: 'I am absolutely convinced that when this process is worked through that Chesterton will come through. I don't believe that money has been laundered through Chesterton.'

Flynn went on to describe himself as an 'unrepentant republican' and said he always would be and would not apologise to anyone for that.

Following Flynn's resignations in the Republic, there was a shock resignation in the North. The chairman of the Policing Board, Sir Desmond Rea, felt he had no alternative but to offer his resignation as a non-executive director of Ivy Wood Properties, a wholly owned subsidiary of Harcourt Developments, a company linked to Phil Flynn.

Sir Desmond had joined the Ivy Wood board in September 2004. The company owns land for development in the Titanic Quarter in the Belfast shipyard complex.

In a statement Sir Desmond said:

> As soon as I had the first indication that there was any link, however tenuous and speculative, between my position as a non-executive director of Ivy Wood Properties Ltd and the widespread coverage around the ongoing policing operations in the Irish Republic, I decided that it would be appropriate for me to stand down from the Ivy Wood Properties Board, which I joined only last September.

Sir Desmond said he knew nothing untoward about Ivy Wood, Harcourt Developments or Phil Flynn.

In his letter of resignation addressed to the chairman of Harcourt Developments, Sir Desmond wrote: 'You will no doubt appreciate that, given my role as the chairman of the Northern Ireland Policing Board, I cannot afford to bring such publicity, however ill-founded, to the door of the Policing Board.'

He said he had no shareholding in either of the two companies and to the best of his knowledge he had never met Phil Flynn.

Next day, Friday 18 February, the spotlight switched briefly to the north-west as police searched premises in Derry linked to the two men arrested at Heuston Station with Bullman. The home of Conor McLaughlin at Woodside Heights was searched as well as a flat above a Sinn Féin office at Strabane Old Road. An officer was injured in this part of the operation as a group of youths threw stones at the PSNI search party.

But it appears that the police raided the wrong house with their warrant to search the property of the other man briefly detained in Dublin, Christopher McElhinney. The occupant of the house told reporters, and the visiting police officers: 'I don't know him. I've never heard of him. I've nothing to do with any political or any other organisation.'

My senior Garda source told me:

When the time was right we intercepted some of the cash at Heuston station in Dublin and we arrested Bullman and two men from Derry. We then asked the PSNI to conduct raids in Derry. The Provos in Derry were shitting themselves because of what they feared could be discovered. But as it happens those raids in Derry produced nothing.

Yet strangely enough, three months later, the PSNI went in again and this time found ledgers and books that dealt with a massive fraud being used by the Provos. This relates to building sites and huge IRA investment in the construction of houses—especially in Donegal . . . but also in the North. There were files all filled with stuff we needed relating to Northern Ireland, the Republic and the UK—stuff about housing developments, housing estates in Donegal for example.

But back to the Garda search operations . . . by close of business on Thursday 17 February, the people of Ireland went to sleep believing they had heard it all for the time being about money laundering and Chesterton Finance . . . but they were wrong.

Friday 18 February brought more surprises. For a start, there were further police raids on the offices of accountants and solicitors in Dublin, Cork, Dun Laoghaire, Portlaoise and Louth. In every office, the police removed computers and documents.

Meanwhile, at Garda headquarters in Dublin the Commissioner, Noel Conroy, was addressing a packed lunchtime news conference and warning that this was an investigation that would take months to conclude. He also urged members of the public to come forward to the Gardaí rather than waiting for the Gardaí to come calling at their door.

The events of the previous forty-eight hours had created a kind of news hysteria. The Garda Commissioner's presence before the mass of microphones and cameras even suggested he was caught up in it all, so unusual was his first address to the media during a 'live' Garda operation.

He also told reporters that the money recovered had 'a subversive involvement'. That position appeared to be underlined later that Friday afternoon when Don Bullman appeared at the Special Criminal Court to face a charge that he was a member of the Real IRA.

Court reporters hung on every word of evidence from the head of the Garda Special Branch, Det. Ch. Supt Philip Kelly. He informed the court that after finding the £54,000 cash in the Daz soapbox at Heuston Station, he suspected the money was part of an IRA money laundering operation.

Ch. Supt Kelly told the court that at the time of Bullman's arrest he was in a Northern Ireland registered car with two men from the North. Along with the Daz packet found on the back seat, he said six mobile phones were also discovered in the car.

Bullman's counsel, Anne Rowland, said her client had two jobs —one as a chef in a nursing home—and worked seventy hours a week. He had never previously been before a court and Ms Rowland said there had been 'prejudicial publicity' about him that could prejudice his trial.

While all this was going on, Gardaí in Cork got an amazing tip-off! Apparently someone in Passage West was burning Northern Bank notes at his home . . . and pieces of the charred notes were to be found near the man's home in Cork Harbour town.

Gardaí searched the house and arrested the man. They believe the man panicked when he saw all the searches and arrests. He placed a substantial amount of Northern notes in his fireplace— possibly as much as £1.5m according to one police source—and set fire to them. But some of the notes went up the chimney before they were burned. Half-burned notes were found in his garden and other bank notes were found inside. They also found between 150-200 heavy calibre bullets thought to be for an AK-47.

But there were still more shocks to come.

Three businessmen contacted Gardaí independently in Cork and handed in cash given to them—they said—by Ted Cunningham. In total, the Gardaí took delivery of £225,000.

The most bizarre episode in this seemingly endless catalogue of money laundering mayhem occurred in Belfast, when £50,000 of stolen Northern Bank notes turned up in a club in the south of the city . . . but it was no ordinary club—it was the sports club used by members of the PSNI at New Forge Lane, off the Malone Road.

It seems a gang of IRA men dressed as athletes sneaked into the club, which is owned by the RUC Athletic Association, and placed the Northern Bank robbery cash in the suspended ceiling of the roof in the men's toilet. The money was stacked in five bundles of £10,000—each bundle in a heat-sealed bag.

The club is not only used by retired and serving police officers, it is also available to members of the public, so security was relatively relaxed.

Police sources said the gang involved was also connected to the bank heist, the 2002 Castlereagh police station break-in and the 1996 car bomb attack on Thiepval Army Barracks in Lisburn, Co. Antrim. Other security sources said the team was trained by the IRA's intelligence chief.

Police regarded this as a stunt by the IRA gang responsible for the robbery. No doubt it gave the robbers a laugh . . . though the police were not amused. But it wasn't quite the final act of this three-day period of intense police activity, which seemed to pile shock upon shock.

A 56-year-old businesswoman was arrested by the Criminal Assets Bureau at a house in Killucan, Co. Westmeath, that had been searched some days earlier. The Gardaí suspected that the woman was involved in the attempts to launder money in Bulgaria. She was questioned for twenty-four hours at Balbriggan Garda station and then released without charge while a file was prepared for the DPP.

She was arrested at a house that had at one time been occupied by Cathy Armstrong, the business partner of Ted Cunningham. The woman is also a business associate of Phil Flynn and it was she who led a seven-strong delegation—including Flynn and Cunningham—to Bulgaria a month before the police raids.

She set up a meeting for the Irish party with Ilia Lingorski, Bulgaria's deputy finance minister. The meeting, held in a restaurant in Sofia, was monitored by agents from the Bulgarian National Security Service.

Detectives involved in the investigation briefed reporters to say they have evidence that the woman, who is believed to be from Northern Ireland, was attempting to launder money from the Northern Bank raid through an established network of Bulgarian business links.

She has extensive business contacts in Bulgaria and first visited the country in 2003. Since then, she has travelled back there at least a dozen times. Gardaí believe she worked on Cunningham's behalf in Bulgaria, and also in Malta and Libya.

The woman had run a series of legitimate businesses and acted as a buyer and seller of properties, including quarries and other business ventures, in Ireland. It was revealed by Gardaí that the woman—along with Flynn and Cunningham—had begun moves to set up three companies in Bulgaria: Alexander Finance; Bulgarian Property & Development; and Addison, all dealing with mortgages and properties.

It was reported that Flynn and Cunningham opened two bank accounts in the Corporate Commercial Bank in Sofia, depositing €1,000 in each account. Subsequently, €55,000 was transferred to a Bulgarian lawyer to set up the three companies.

Flynn and Cunningham had travelled to Sofia with a party of four which included Denis O'Connell—someone with considerable experience of investing in Eastern Europe property. The rest of the party—a German-based lawyer with a practice in Sofia, an international consultant and the Irish businesswoman —met with auctioneers, property developers and bankers.

Even the doors of government opened to them, no doubt helped along by Flynn's stature as chairman of a valuable British-owned bank. And that's how Flynn and Cunningham were able to met with Ilia Lingorski, Bulgaria's deputy finance minister responsible for foreign inward investment.

After the Garda Commissioner's press conference on the Friday, the press picked up the search for information. That weekend's newspapers featured extensive coverage of the Garda operation, with particular focus on Phil Flynn.

Flynn told reporters that he had hoped to set up a financial company, but it was all totally innocent: he wanted to organise a company like Cunningham's Chesterton Finance in Bulgaria or establish a mortgage company. He said he had canvassed many business people and 'carried a brief for a number of business people'.

One Irish newspaper, the *Sunday Business Post*, made another stunning discovery. It received information from a Bulgarian government source about the visit by the Irish property speculators, who apparently claimed that the four Irish individuals represented a financial institution registered in Amsterdam with capital of roughly €14 million. But Phil Flynn said he had no idea what they were referring to.

Phil Flynn's transformation from a republican on the outside of Ireland's establishment to a formidable player within establishment circles is clear. As a highly regarded government adviser, he could count Taoiseach Bertie Ahern among his friends. Other government figures have reason to be grateful to Flynn for helping resolve industrial disputes.

But while heading the government's decentralisation programme and while chairman of the Bank of Scotland (Ireland), Flynn—on his own admission—was acting as an adviser to Sinn Féin on how it could go about overhauling its party structure.

While the Irish government was acknowledging the IRA's role in criminal activities—like the Northern Bank robbery—the man advising the IRA's political wing was still operating closely with government figures in his role on the decentralisation programme.

When news broke about his involvement with the Garda investigation into an IRA money laundering operation, it raised serious questions amongst Flynn's political allies and business associates about his transition from republican activist to wealthy establishment figure. Certainly, politically the question is about whether or not Flynn had ever truly severed his links with the republican movement or indeed whether or not he had ever stopped working for the republican cause.

Unionists were quick to exploit the opportunity. Ulster Unionist peer Lord Laird used parliamentary privilege to make allegations relating to Phil Flynn. He also accused the Taoiseach of betraying his own country by allowing Flynn to remain a close adviser while knowing he was still associating with senior IRA figures.

Lord Laird claimed Gardaí had seen Brian Keenan, whom he described as a member of the IRA Army Council, staying for some time at Flynn's home in Dublin and he further alleged: 'They also observed Slab Murphy, the IRA army chief of staff, meeting Flynn on a regular basis.'

He described Flynn as being a management consultant to the IRA since 2004. The peer also claimed that Flynn had been part of the Taoiseach's peace talks team that had visited British Prime Minister Tony Blair at No. 10 Downing Street. Tony Blair refused to deny claims that Flynn had visited No. 10.

Flynn challenged Lord Laird to make his allegations outside Parliament when he said: 'It would be very useful, once and for all, for me to be able to deal with this if he repeated it outside the House. Then we could establish the facts. He doesn't have to establish the facts in Parliament. Outside the House he does.'

Flynn added that he had no comment to make on the detail of Lord Laird's statement: 'Otherwise I would just be giving credence to lies.'

As the political temperature rose for the Taoiseach, an Irish government spokesman issued a statement: 'Mr Flynn was never part of any Irish government delegation to Downing Street.' But the spokesman could not be drawn on the possibility that Flynn had been there in another capacity. That careful wording leaves the way open to consider that Flynn may have been part of a Sinn Féin delegation at a time when he was chairman of the Irish government's decentralisation committee. A spokesman for the British Prime Minister simply refused to deny that Flynn had visited No. 10.

Outside parliamentary privilege, Lord Laird said he had first raised the question of Flynn's involvement with the Irish government in peace talks as early as 29 April 2005 when he contacted the Taoiseach's office. But he said he had received no reply in spite of repeated attempts to get one.

Flynn was also the subject of a question in the House of

Commons in February 2004 when Ulster Unionist MP David Burnside asked the then Secretary of State Paul Murphy what discussions had taken place between Northern Ireland government departments and agencies with Phil Flynn since 1998.

Murphy told Burnside: 'No records exist of discussions between Mr Phil Flynn of Harcourt Developments and the Northern Ireland Office or the Northern Ireland departments and agencies.'

Flynn was a director of Harcourt Developments, and Burnside was not prepared to let the matter go. He then asked the Secretary of State for Northern Ireland what discussions had taken place between Northern Ireland government departments and agencies and Harcourt Developments since 1998.

It was at this point that Paul Murphy revealed that a number of Northern Ireland departments and agencies had had talks with Harcourt Developments in relation to the development of a number of locations. He added: 'Records indicate that the Northern Ireland Office has had no discussions with the company.'

All of which prompted the Republic's Justice Minister Michael McDowell to suggest Flynn should be tried for spying!

But others focused on the Bulgarian connections. DUP MEP Jim Allister raised a question in the European Parliament. The former communist state is scheduled to become a European Union member in 2007 and Allister wanted to know if the state had any money laundering legislation.

The answer was that only after a crime is proven can a prosecution for money laundering begin. And no one had ever been convicted of the offence.

This, for Allister, explained the IRA interest in investing in businesses over there. He said:

> This proves that Bulgaria is indeed a ready-made haven for money laundering operations. The commission has identified a major gap in Bulgaria's criminal justice system and the obvious attraction for gangster organisations like the IRA.

The absence of a proper system of anti-terrorism laws confirms me in my decision to vote against Bulgarian membership of the EU. It is an unhappy prospect that come January 2007, Bulgaria with its lax approach to terrorism will be a full member of the EU—with all the consequences for free movement of goods, services and people.

The European Commission believes Bulgaria is making progress in combating money laundering whilst also admitting that there is no judicial practice of prosecuting money laundering as a stand-alone criminal offence.

The Commission stated:

> Only when the offence is proven can a prosecution for money laundering start. Until today, no convictions for money laundering have been reported in Bulgaria. The Commission will, therefore, continue to follow closely the implementation of the adopted framework in order to ensure that cases of money laundering and terrorism financing are effectively prosecuted and convictions eventually delivered by Bulgarian courts.

If the European Commission's statement is correct, it renders dubious, to say the least, a claim by the Bulgarian authorities that it had conducted an investigation into the Irish money laundering allegations and concluded there was no evidence of it.

But, certainly, the Bulgarian connections fascinate the Gardaí. Officers have been sent there to find out for themselves exactly what was going on there.

In the meantime, at home the Garda investigation ran out of its seemingly endless supply of daily news sensations. So as media interest waned a little, the Gardaí and the PSNI continued to investigate the Cork connections to what they firmly believed was an IRA money laundering operation—their aim to produce a file for the Director of Public Prosecutions in Dublin.

The Gardaí believe that around £5m of the Northern Bank cash had found its way to Cork—at least they believe they can account for that amount.

My senior Garda source told me that for many months prior to this operation, there was an ongoing investigation into the activities of the IRA. He said:

> The IRA has an extremely sophisticated money gathering operation and is very capable of getting into profit through a whole range of business operations—pubs owned by former Army Council members, for example, buying up pockets of land and developing it for housing. The money gives the Provos great power. And they have been manipulating the system down South for years.

Gerry Adams was in Spain on a book promotion tour as details of the Garda operation emerged. He said Sinn Féin was not involved in any money laundering activities and he said he had seen or heard nothing at this time to make him change his view that the IRA was not responsible for the Northern Bank raid.

Pressed to say what would happen if evidence emerged that linked the IRA to the robbery, he said: 'Such a serious situation as you are suggesting might emerge will take very serious reflection by me and others who are in the leadership of Sinn Féin.'

The Sinn Féin president said he was not going to make a knee-jerk reaction but would face up to such issues if they emerged, adding: 'I want to see a united Ireland. I don't want to be tainted with criminality. I don't want anybody near me who is involved in criminality.'

He totally rejected as 'party political' comments made by Justice Minister Michael McDowell that the Provisional movement was a 'colossal crime machine laundering huge sums of money'.

—

It was not just at home that the Northern Bank robbers attempted to launder their cash. The police believe that the

Cheltenham race festival in March 2005 was used to 'cleanse' hundreds of thousands of pounds—and possibly even millions.

Cheltenham attracts 200,000 people—a quarter of them Irish. In the region of £40m is spent each year in bets and as much as £1.5m cash is bet on each race. Prior to the event there were warnings that Northern Bank cash would be used there— including one from the chief of Ireland's Criminal Assets Bureau, Ch. Supt Felix McKenna.

But in spite of the warnings, police later identified that there had been a disproportionate amount of Northern Ireland sterling passed at the four-day festival and they link that to the laundering of cash stolen in the bank heist.

Meanwhile, as the Gardaí continued their investigations in the South and as the politicians made political capital out of Sinn Féin's discomfort, up North the money laundering operation was going on quietly and efficiently right under the noses of the Northern Bank.

I made contact with a man who wanted to tip me off about the way the laundering was taking place. It involves the Chinese community in one area of Belfast.

He told me:

I know about a company that trades with the Chinese/Asian business communities in Belfast. The Chinese deal in cash. This company sells its products to the Chinese. I don't want to identify either the company or what it sells.

But I can tell you that something odd has been happening since the Northern Bank robbery. Normally, the breakdown in the notes handed over [to this company] by the Chinese— and they are always dirty and often smelly and look as though they have been curled up—would consist of 40 per cent Northern Bank; 40 per cent Ulster Bank and the remainder in other denominations from other banks. That would be the normal breakdown.

But recently there has been a big increase in Northern Bank notes . . . and grade 'A' notes at that. Having once worked in a bank, I know something about how notes are graded.

What we are talking about here are grade 'A' notes—used notes considered to be in good enough condition to be used in the ATMs. And once these notes are graded and bound together in the cash centre, they are marked . . . you can see the mark drawn down along the ends of the notes when they are packed together and wrapped.

So now, when these notes are counted for the bank you can see the mark. It is fairly clear that these are Northern Bank stolen notes. When they are taken to the bank, the Northern, for lodgement I keep waiting to hear that the bank teller has finally caught on. I keep thinking the person lodging the cash is going to get a tap on the shoulder or be asked by the teller to wait just a moment as he or she heads off to alert other bank staff.

But the tellers are too busy making sure the amounts tally to appear to notice the notes or even be suspicious about them. Bank staff employed at the counter lack the experience to notice. There's one young girl who is only interested in making sure that if his lodgement slip says £5,000, that she counts £5,000 in cash to keep her tally correct at the end of the day.

And yet Northern bank branches are constantly being reminded that anyone coming in with more than £250 in old notes cannot have it exchanged for cash even if they have an account. This money has to be lodged into the account. Any sums above that must also be lodged. There are very strict rules following the robbery.

The Chinese are clearly doing a deal with republicans to launder the stolen cash. The way it would work is that the Provos would proffer £5,000 to the Chinese and ask for £4,000 or £4,500—leaving the Chinese to make a profit.

What is also interesting about the Chinese is that they haggle over every penny. That has been the experience of most companies doing business with them. They argue and hustle to get the best value they can for their cash. But since the laundering of money began, they no longer bother to haggle. That's more evidence that the Chinese are 'making a buck' through the transactions.

It would appear that the Northern Bank knew exactly how much money had been stolen but was blissfully unaware of the robbers' use of this Chinese laundering process. The bank seemed to be relying on the fact that it had chosen to re-issue its bank notes with a different design as a means of frustrating the robbery gang.

This wasn't just the worst robbery in the history of the Northern Bank, it was the worst in British history—up to that time.

07 | KILLING THE 'CASH COW'

'National Australia Bank was attuned to what was going on globally in the financial world and that drove changes for them and as I said earlier the only criticism is that perhaps they may have gone too fast. The strategy imperatives for the National Australia Bank were in Great Britain, not here. They did not invest money here. There's no doubt about that.'—FORMER NORTHERN BANK MANAGEMENT OFFICIAL

—

There is never a good time for a bank to suffer the financial loss and embarrassment of a robbery. But for the Australian owners of the Northern Bank, the then biggest cash robbery in British history could not have come at a worse time.

With financial problems at home in Australia and trouble with its other investments in the United States, National Australia Bank had decided to capitalise on its Irish investment. The trouble was that the ink was barely dry on the contract of sale to the Danish bank Danske. The transfer of ownership was scheduled to happen the following spring.

The Northern Bank had provided the Australians with consistently good profits throughout their seventeen years in ownership and now it had been sold for around nine times what they had paid for it.

But, critically, with £26m missing from its vaults, questions were now being asked about the Australians' stewardship of the bank and the way they had handled security arrangements.

For almost two hundred years the Northern Bank had survived without any scandal on this scale. The official records show that the Northern Bank was founded in 1824 but unofficially it actually began business as a small private bank in 1809. With financial prudence, the Northern Bank built up a sound customer base and steadily grew into the biggest bank in Northern Ireland—becoming so successful that in 1965 it became part of the largest bank in the world, the Midland. But when the Midland got into financial difficulties in the 1980s with the bad debts it inherited with its purchase of the Crocker Bank in the United States, it badly needed to generate fresh income. The decision was made to sell the Northern Bank—described by one financier as the Midland's 'family silver'—to the National Australia Bank for £408m cash.

That £408m gave the Australians ownership of the Midland's three subsidiary banks in Scotland and Ireland—the Clydesdale, the Northern and Northern Bank (Ireland), which almost immediately became National Irish Bank (NIB).

As a former leading official in the Northern Bank told me, the Australians were reluctant to become involved in Ireland at all:

National Australia Bank actually wanted only to buy the Clydesdale Bank but were told they had to take the Irish banks as well, and National Australia's Chief Executive in Melbourne, Nobby Clark, told us that from day one. He only had us for a few months and he was describing the Northern Bank as the jewel in the crown. He said the Midland did not know what it was missing. The Northern was a good return on the capital . . . a good investment.

A senior Midland Bank official, now retired, told me how he remembers the purchase by the Australians:

I was a regional director of the Midland Bank—on secondment—based in London when the Aussies bought the Northern and the Clydesdale. I was approached to come over to Northern Ireland. Of course, I was not party to the discussions or the rationale to take over the bank.

The chairman of the National Australia Bank would come

over to London two or three times a year and he had breakfast or lunch with the Midland Bank Chairman, also an Aussie. At the time the Midland had taken big losses on the Crocker Bank in California. In order to repair the balance sheets, it was decided by the Midland to sell off the Northern Bank and the Clydesdale, and it was at least a means of improving the look of the annual returns.

Staff at the Northern Bank had been expecting news of a takeover for some time before the announcement in 1987. The only surprise was the identity of the new owners. It had been widely anticipated that a European bank was most likely to buy the Northern Bank.

At first, according to another former Northern Bank management figure, the new owners indicated that there would be few changes:

> Nobby Clark was head of the National Bank of Australia (NAB). He was their Chief Executive based at the bank's headquarters in Melbourne. When the takeover happened, he called all senior management into the boardroom. He told us: 'We will not interfere with you. You are profitable and working well and we will not interfere as long as you go on producing profits.' He was a gentleman. And he did let us get on with our work. Clark would come over to Belfast once a year when he was in London.
>
> The Northern Bank board remained intact and continued to function, although I think the NAB had someone on the board, or at least they had an alternative person who travelled over to represent the person in Australia who couldn't obviously come to every meeting. But when Clark retired some three or four years later, things began to change when his replacement, Don Argus, took over.

That the Australians initially impressed Northern Bank staff with their easy-going approach cannot be overstated. Everyone I spoke to recalled the good times. As this former senior official in the

Northern told me: 'I found the Australians very efficient and was certainly impressed by them. With the time difference, I would send stuff to Australia and would find it dealt with by the time I got back in next morning. They certainly moved quickly.'

The Australian purchase of the Northern Bank was finalised in October 1987. Soon staff at the Northern were preparing to take over functions that previously had been the sole preserve of the Midland Bank—such as leasing, factoring and selling insurance services.

The Northern was told to adopt the 'National' business method, which meant re-organising the bank's services into three sectors—retail, business and premium. One former senior Northern Bank official who was deeply involved in helping the Australians make a smooth transition into Northern Bank ownership recalled:

After the takeover by National Australia Bank, they ran the Northern and the Clydesdale as separate units. They told us they wanted us to go on as we had been . . . but only to do it better to bring in bigger profits. They recognised that we had a strong brand name. Under Nobby Clark we ran our own show. The National Australia Bank set targets and we met them and our profits were good.

Things began to change when Clark retired and Don Argus took over and he had a different view and it was influenced by business school management and consultancy speak. They looked at the whole UK set-up with three banks—the Northern, the National Irish Bank and the Clydesdale—and they were trying to manage it as one unit. Banking is all about the customer interface. Once they had acquired the Yorkshire Bank as well, they had four separate banks with four separate back office activities to deal with, and what they wanted to do was to bring as much of that activity into one central operation. Their attitude to cash operations was crucial.

Each bank had to operate within its legal entity but there were background operations that could be centralised. Now these changes were in my opinion necessary. The Northern

Bank could not continue as it was because there were compelling changes in the world of banking.

One former management figure told me:

When Don Argus took over as Chief Executive, nothing changed immediately but he did interfere more and more in the routine of the banks. After I retired I was at Jakarta airport and I picked up the *Australian Business Magazine* and in an article he [Argus] was discussing the European banks the National Australia Bank owned and in this article Argus criticised the Northern Bank computer system. He boasted he would put in the Australian system.

But the computer system did not change under Argus. A new system for the entire group was considered, but Argus would not approve the finance necessary for the European banks.

There was no real attempt to invest in the Northern by the Australians. Consider this comment from a current employee, made after the Australians sold to the Danes:

The Aussies did not invest in Northern Bank or National Irish Bank. There's not a single branch of the Northern Bank that has a PC. The bank's branches are still back in the seventies, technically speaking. Now Danske, the new owners, are having to spend substantial sums to upgrade the bank's computer system and all its branches. It might be as much as £100m.

And Danske have set about this computer revolution with some degree of determination and relish. One Northern Bank employee told me:

Danske are so committed to improving IT skills that they have provided everyone with a laptop and printer for their homes. Every computer has Windows XP. People are encouraged to use them to improve their skills and to learn about the Internet. In fact, they are using the Internet as a means of doing their examinations so they eventually end up with what is an international driving licence. So everyone will be computer literate and ready for the new challenges in the workplace.

Another Northern Bank employee told me that on a recent visit to a branch of the National Irish Bank in Donegal, he saw an antiquated computer system in use. 'You remember those early computers with the green coloured screens?' he asked. 'Well, that's what they were using there. It is a ridiculous situation. In this day and age to have people still using such ancient equipment is a disgrace and lets you know just how little the Australians were prepared to invest in their Irish banking operations.'

But it wasn't just in Ireland that there was evidence of a lack of investment. Consider this evidence from a current employee:

During one visit of the National Australia Bank board to Britain and Ireland, one of the board members was amazed to see that the computer system at the Yorkshire Bank was so antiquated, he remarked that it might be worth something if only to place in a museum to let people see how things used to be in the seventies. The Aussies raped businesses they controlled throughout Europe just in the same way as the Romans had done centuries before. The Northern Bank was left in a state of serious decline. There just was no investment.

And yet there are others who worked at senior levels in the Northern Bank who feel such criticism is undeserved:

National Australia Bank Europe centralised management and administration so that Glasgow became the location where the other banks reported to, even though they remained domiciled in Ireland.

Three or four years ago the support areas, while still in the legal entity of the bank, began reporting to Glasgow. Now I was not the line manager; I became their customer. We could merge functions like mortgage operations and it was successful and made business sense. The only thing that might upset people in the bank was the speed with which these changes were made.

Nobby Clark was the visionary. He had outgrown Australia with its population of 15–16 million where the National Australia Bank had been a conservative bank that did not get caught up in property lending and Third World poverty like other banks in Australia. They lost money on those enterprises . . . but National Australia Bank resisted the temptation to go that way . . . so they moved swiftly to maximise their investment here.

Each of the banks had their own cheque clearing; cash centres; properties and administration. The National Australia Bank plan was to centralise what they could and reduce outgoings. So they merged a lot of those functions.

But even some of the more pro-Australian former managers felt there was a lack of investment in the Northern. One such figure expressed his opinion this way:

National Australia Bank was first to face the significant re-structuring needed in banking in Ireland and they did it without compulsory redundancies. In fact, there have only been 200/300 jobs lost. Think of the 1,700 job losses just announced by the Bank of Ireland.

A lot of the jobs are no longer part of the Northern Bank because of those functions that have moved to Scotland with National Australia Bank Europe . . . the centralising stuff from the branches. This gave the bank an economy of scale to staff and at the same time improved services. Ordering chequebooks or contacting your branch is done through Glasgow now.

National Australia Bank was attuned to what was going on globally in the financial world and that drove changes for them and, as I said earlier, the only criticism is that perhaps they may have gone too fast.

The strategy imperatives for the National Australia Bank were in Great Britain, not here. They did not invest money here. There's no doubt about that. So Danske will invest heavily here and they will have a different attitude.

Not only do the Australians stand accused of failing to invest, they also stand accused of adopting business practices that disadvantaged the bank in competing with other financial institutions, with the result that the Northern Bank lost customers, profits and a large portion of its share of business.

Ben Wilson, an experienced accountant who spent years with the renowned firm of accountants KPMG, argues that the Australian style of global banking left the Northern Bank in a financially weak position. He was highly critical of the way the National Australia Bank ran its corporate business affairs:

> The arrival of National Australia Bank signalled a contraction of the Northern Bank's corporate business. It became difficult to obtain substantial corporate loans—in excess of £10m—with Aussie approval. Great opportunities were to bypass Northern Ireland businessmen as the Northern Bank came under the influence and control of the Australians.

Support for Ben Wilson's views comes from someone who once worked for the Northern Bank and who witnessed first-hand the way in which the Australian owners gradually eroded the bank's corporate business. He told me:

> The Australians cost the Northern Bank millions in business. After Nobby Clark retired, Don Argus changed the shape of banking at the Northern. We were no long able to compete for corporate business. The way the Australians ran our affairs had the effect of curtailing our opportunities to become involved with local businessmen who had an empathy with the local community. Decisions on corporate business policy were apparently being taken in Melbourne, probably by some 27-year-old business graduate who had no feeling for the Northern Ireland community, no understanding of the way people here did business.

Like every other former Northern Bank manager or executive I interviewed, this individual felt a loyalty to the 'old' Northern Bank—the bank that had existed very profitably and successfully before the arrival of the Australians. But even his anger at the way the Australians managed the bank and used it for its profits would not entice him to speak out publicly.

Nonetheless, like so many other former employees, he was highly critical of the way the bank was manipulated by the Australians. He had tales of businessmen coming with proposals to the Northern Bank for investment projects. His tales are touched by frustration that he was unable to help.

'It was a terrible time,' he said. 'We had so many restrictions that it became impossible to compete. Our ability to approve loans was basically taken away from us. We could only approve up to £2.5m locally and if we wanted anything above that to be sanctioned, we had to refer to the credit committee in Glasgow. Anything above £10m had to be referred to Melbourne.'

The net effect of this policy was to undermine the local banking expertise that was available in the Northern. The kind of expertise that had been the foundation of the bank's continued good fortune and profitability. Under Aussie rules that expertise counted for nothing.

Ben Wilson cited the case of Belfast International Airport as an example of an opportunity lost to local businessmen and the Northern Bank. 'The International Airport needed substantial funding to keep control of the airport in Northern Ireland,' he said, 'but the Northern Bank could not give that commitment. Mind you, other banks failed to take up the opportunity and we all know that after only two years, huge profits were made on the resale of the airport.'

My banking source was able to confirm the airport story. He said there was one very simple explanation as to why the Northern Bank could not help:

We were ordered not to become involved in MBOS [management buy outs]. The Australians would not fund such enterprises. This is the way they missed out on

Aldergrove airport. The Northern Bank managers in corporate lending asked the Australians a couple of times to reconsider the airport, but like so many other cases put to them, the answer was no.

Indeed, it wasn't just MBOs that were rejected by the Australians. My contact knew of cases that qualified on every level—where the experts in the Northern Bank considered that the risk was covered and therefore minimal and that the debt could be serviced—were turned down in Melbourne.

Good customers who dealt regularly with the Northern Bank suddenly found themselves being turned away—and sometimes the Northern Bank person they dealt with became so frustrated with the attitude of the Australians in Melbourne that he or she would recommend the customer to try elsewhere. Often the beneficiary of this lacking in the Northern Bank was the Anglo-Irish Bank.

The long-term effect of this policy was devastating, according to Northern Bank sources. One said:

We drove our customers away. People who had always been with the Northern and who had completed many business transactions satisfactorily now found that we were no longer the bank that likes to say 'Yes'. That was once our advertising slogan: the bank that likes to say 'Yes'. But now we had become that bank that says 'No' to perfectly good, viable propositions. Other banks picked up our slack and benefited from our failure to work with the local business community.

Our people were on the ground and had an empathy and understanding of local business affairs. We lived in the community. But we lost the power of attorney when making banking decisions on potential business opportunities. We had effectively been neutered by the Australians.

Driving customers away had consequences. The Northern Bank was rapidly disappearing down the charts as one of the leading banks in Northern Ireland.

The failure to invest and the corporate business strategy that drove customers away raised crucial questions about the commitment of the National Australian Bank to not only the Northern Bank but to Northern Ireland.

I visited Companies House in Belfast to collect the Northern Bank's annual accounts from 1986 to 2004 . . . which covers the seventeen years the Australians had control of the Northern Bank. Ben Wilson agreed to cast his expert eye over the figures and produce some kind of analysis that would demonstrate how the Northern Bank performed for the Australians. The figures are quite startling.

This is how Ben Wilson summed them up:

> The profit chart sets out the excellent profitability of the Northern Bank over nineteen years and it also shows the dividends taken by National Australia Bank, which, in the early years, were modest but in the latter years were maximised so much that all after-tax profits were taken by way of dividend with nothing put into reserves.
>
> In addition, some special dividends were taken in 1987 of £61m and in 1992 of £100m and from 2000 to 2004, after-tax profits were extracted totalling £312m. It was a different picture for the bank's deposit customers with rates as low as .1% compared to 100% taken by the owners, the Australians.

But one former Northern Bank executive I interviewed bristled angrily when discussing the question of profits and how the Australians used them. He was particularly upset when he heard people say National Australia Bank only came to Northern Ireland to asset-strip the Northern Bank. This is what he said:

> National Australia Bank had a very professional bank here [the Northern], regarded as a 'cash cow'. There was more money going out in dividends than was being invested. But what's wrong with that? Any large organisation is entitled to do as it pleases with its profits—that's why it acquires businesses—to make profit.

What's wrong with that, according to so many others who worked at the Northern Bank, is that the Australians used the Northern to prop up their other failed and, as we will discover later, sometimes corrupt business enterprises.

That's why the same executive quoted above offered this thought about the years the Australians had control of the Northern: 'In the early years it was good to work for National Australia Bank, but as National Australia came under increasing pressure back in Australia, then the work here became more pressurised as well.'

Of course there was pressure from a bank that was operating out of control and that was in deep financial trouble both at home in Australia and in the United States. So that pressure he refers to was to maintain and improve profits at almost any cost. And in the latter years, the Australians needed as much profit as they could muster to try to cover the cracks and their tracks in the United States and corrupt practices in Australia and—as it happens—in the Republic of Ireland as well.

The imperative for the National Australia Bank at its headquarters in Melbourne was to milk as much as they could from whatever cash cow they could find—and the Northern Bank was one of those cash cows.

As one former Northern Bank official explained:

Everything the Australians did in Northern Ireland was to increase profits for them—not to produce profits for investment and improvement of the existing bank here. They even sold property to increase profits. And they were constantly looking for ways to save money to push the profits even higher.

A number of the properties sold off were in Belfast and included Waring Street—the former head office of the Belfast Banking Company, Victoria Street and Griffin House—the office block in Bedford Street in the city centre opposite the headquarters where the raid took place. To replace those properties closed, the Australians leased other premises.

Apparently, under National Australia Bank's own credit policy it would be mandatory to have a covenant in their facility letter insisting that a minimum of 20 per cent of profits are utilised for reinvestment. There was little sign of this policy in their Irish operations.

As far as Ben Wilson is concerned, the way the Australians managed their affairs at the Northern Bank is a matter of some concern. He poses a number of serious questions:

> So where was the Bank of England? Silent or uninterested? Did they even know the Australians had taken out about three-quarters of a billion [£750 million] in dividends over the eighteen years?
>
> Was the Bank of England protecting the financial strength of leading Northern Ireland financial institutions? Did they use their moderating and controlling hand?
>
> Of course they will argue that the Australians were legally entitled to take out or dividend up all after-tax profits under Company Law—and so they were. But in the process, was the Northern Bank financially weakened? Would an independent observer say the Australians acted in a fair and reasonable capacity or were they only in Northern Ireland to milk the cow?
>
> What a bank the Northern has proved to be—it has supported two lame ducks, the Midland Bank's USA disastrous venture and the National Australia Bank's foreign exchange fraud and their disastrous American venture.

The Australians were undoubtedly reluctant owners of the Northern Bank. Their main interest in Europe was to establish a hold in England and Scotland. But at the end of the day, the Northern Bank was a cash cow that helped bail them out of trouble in the same way it had helped the Midland Bank.

Ben Wilson's questions come from a man who is clearly upset by the way the Australians traded in Northern Ireland. Others felt just as strongly—mainly those who worked there and who watched as the Northern Bank's prestige suffered and their working environment deteriorated.

Another retired Northern Bank official told me:

> There was a period in the last five to eight years when there
> was no investment here and the squeeze was on to improve
> profits and improve the cost/income ratio. When National
> Australia Bank bought Northern Bank they were the third
> largest bank in Australia. But then they built up their business
> to become the biggest company in Australia. They have lost a
> bit of ground today after some difficult times because of the
> high standards they set and they had to go on and on
> improving and most of their investment was on the home
> market in Australia with less in Europe. Their profits fell by 20
> per cent—the only bank in Australia not to improve on
> profits.

National Australia Bank in Australia had by then become
involved in corrupt practices that caused a scandal and cost the
bank millions. In fact, National Australia Bank was not being run
properly. It was, to use the words of the Australian financial
watchdog, a bank that 'failed at every level'. It was a bank out of
control.

And on foreign shores the bank had become somewhat
accustomed to making losses on bad judgements. Take the United
States for example. The Australians had a couple of failures there
that cost them millions.

So what had gone wrong?

The bank should have had sufficient warning that its checks
and controls were not in order but apparently did not learn from
the painful experiences in America.

During the 1980s National Australia Bank had been praised by
analysts and the media for avoiding the worst of the domestic
lending excesses in Australia. At the time the bank had built up
the largest United States branch network of any of the Australian
banks.

By 1989 National Australian Bank had assets in America worth
Aus$4bn. That was around 5 per cent of the company's balance

sheet. But the US business had a pre-tax loss of Aus$12m in that year.

There followed a period of contraction in the United States that saw the assets drop to just 1.5 per cent of the balance sheet and the closure of branches in Atlanta, Chicago, Dallas, Houston and San Francisco. However, these actions could not stem the losses, which in 1990 amounted to Aus$24m and Aus$14m in 1991.

In November 1995, National Australia Bank went on the offensive again in the United States, buying the Michigan National Bank for Aus$2.1bn.

Two years later, the Australians acquired HomeSide—a mortgage servicing company. But it wasn't long before National Australia Bank's Chief Executive Frank Cicutto was reporting huge losses . . . Aus$4bn in fact.

So in this rarefied world of global banking, if you manage the risks badly it can spell disaster. In recent years some of these have been highlighted because of the spectacular collapse of banking institutions such as Barings or the corporate collapses such as Enron. In the case of the corporate failings, the focus falls on the bank's exposure to those companies and the extent of their bad debt provision.

National Australia Bank appears to be good at looking at the books of their proposed acquisitions during the due diligence process and raising provisions. That way it effectively drives down the cost of the purchase. But when it comes to making provisions for their own bad debt?

This lack of checks and controls appears to be a common theme in the problems that the National Australia Bank has faced in the past decade.

So while the Northern Bank continued to perform profitably, the National Australia Bank was losing millions in the United States. The pressure was on the board of the bank to stop haemorrhaging money. The screw was being applied in Belfast and Dublin to keep increasing profits . . . and in the Republic the outcome was to prove disastrous.

08 THE BANK ROBBERS

'Most people will be very cynical of a bank which became aware eight or nine years ago that money was being taken from its clients in some of its branches, which concealed this fact, which made no effort to repay the money in question and which issued a very limp apology only after these facts became public.'—TÁNAISTE MARY HARNEY ANNOUNCING INQUIRIES INTO NATIONAL IRISH BANK FOR TAX EVASION AND OVER CHARGING

—

Dominic welcomed his transfer from urban banking to a rural branch of the National Irish Bank. But he did not like what he saw at his new branch.

Dominic—not his real name—does not want to be identified publicly. And he did not want to be identified with the established practices at his new branch: 'I saw accounts facing charges that should never have been applied. These were perfectly healthy accounts where there should have been no charges.'

Dominic was shocked. 'I declined to take part in this charade,' he told me. 'Other customers were being overcharged for failing to keep their accounts in order. Yes, we did have charges we could apply, but I thought our staff were being over-zealous.'

Dominic was not alone. Although he did not know it at the time, the practice of overcharging was not restricted to his branch —it was, in fact, much more widespread.

But in 1998 there was someone else who worked in the National Irish Bank who decided that it was time to do something about the bank's improper practice. It was this someone who decided to become a whistle-blower . . . it was this someone who made contact with RTÉ. The consequences were to be far-reaching.

The full extent of the overcharging only became apparent to the public when RTÉ reported on 25 March 1998 that National Irish Bank had been involved in the practice. A number of branches were identified—Carrick-on-Shannon, Walkinstown, Cork and Carndonagh. The bank stood accused of 'loading' accounts without legitimate reason and without the knowledge of the customer concerned. Two days before the programme was due to air, the bank had received a letter from the broadcaster seeking comment, and management prepared a statement.

This wasn't the first time RTÉ had done a report on questionable business practices at the National Irish Bank. Two months earlier RTÉ had raised the first whiff of scandal at the bank. This earlier report—broadcast on 23 January 1998—had accused National Irish Bank of marketing an Isle of Man investment product—thereby offering customers an opportunity to evade revenue payments.

The day after the programme was aired on 25 March, the Revenue Commissioners and the Central Bank of Ireland announced investigations—as did the National Irish Bank itself. The Tánaiste Mary Harney said she might consider appointing an official to investigate National Irish Banks under the Companies Act.

As Minister for Enterprise, Trade and Employment, Mary Harney spoke in the Seanad Éireann on 26 March. She did not mince her words:

> The report last night on RTÉ's six o'clock news contained the most damning allegations ever made against an Irish clearing bank. The fact that National Irish Bank has confirmed the substance of the allegations made by RTÉ is shocking.
>
> Most people will be amazed to hear that the bank took money from its customers, that it concealed that fact from them and that it failed to repay the money. People will be shocked to know that it happened eight or nine years ago.

It is worth reading into the record the statement made last night by National Irish Bank. It began by saying that the incidents referred to go back many years and do not reflect current practices. It states that they were practised: '. . . in a small number of branches and in a limited number of accounts. It occurred in the late 1980s and early 1990s. We accept that customers affected by the unauthorised practice were not advised of it and were not offered recompense at that time. The Bank regrets this. National Irish Bank will seek to identify such accounts and undertakes to reimburse any customers so affected.' Most people will be very cynical of a bank which became aware eight or nine years ago that money was being taken from its clients in some of its branches, which concealed this fact, which made no effort to repay the money in question and which issued a very limp apology only after these facts became public.

And she wasn't finished with the National Irish Bank. The Tánaiste went on:

Banks command enormous trust in this economy. When people place their money in a licensed bank they expect it to be safe. It is important we have trust in the banking system. The allegations are seriously damaging for the banking industry, for industry generally and for the international reputation of Ireland. It is fair to say that we have successfully marketed the International Financial Services Centre on the basis that Ireland is a very good place for a bank or financial institution to operate in. It is a serious state of affairs when the trust between a bank and its customers breaks down.

When we became aware in January of the allegations surrounding the management of National Irish Bank's insurance policies, we wrote to the bank, received a response and referred that response to the Attorney General for advice and subsequently to independent senior counsel. That became available on March 10 and it advised a certain course of action.

The course of action was to go to the High Court in Dublin and apply for the appointment of an inspector or team to investigate the National Irish Bank and its relationship with Clerical Medical Insurance. The Clerical Medical product being touted and sold by the bank was technically an insurance product that was not authorised for sale in Ireland.

So, the combined impact of these two RTÉ stories was to cause National Irish Bank enormous public distress that would evolve into a major scandal with dire consequences for the bank.

So sensitive did National Irish Bank feel about its offshore business revenue that it turned, in February 1998, to the courts to try to prevent RTÉ from publishing what it regarded as confidential information. It was an action the bank lost. The Supreme Court ruled on 21 March that RTÉ could go ahead and publish whatever information it had in its possession.

On 21 March, an authorised officer—Martin Cosgrove—was appointed to National Irish Bank to investigate its insurance business.

Four days later, on 25 March, as Ireland's national broadcaster informed the public about National Irish Bank's overcharging of fees and interest, the Cabinet met to discuss the issue and National Irish Bank went public to promise to pay back the money it had taken.

National Irish Bank stood in the dock of public contempt. Try as the bank did to diminish the impact, there was no let-up in the depth of public and government anger.

National Irish Bank was now on the defensive, as the public outcry over their actions grew louder. The omens were not good for the bank and its senior management.

Two days after the overcharging story, on 27 March, the former National Irish Bank Chief Executive Jim Lacey—sacked by the bank in 1994—resigned from the boards of two State companies. There was a sense of foreboding.

At National Irish Bank headquarters, executives were facing increasingly uncomfortable questions from the government about how the bank was running its affairs.

The Tánaiste finally announced on 30 March that two

inspectors—former Supreme Court judge John Blayney and bank expert Tom Grace—had been appointed by the High Court on her application to investigate the allegations of overcharging as well as the allegations that the bank was involved in facilitating tax evasion.

Meanwhile, on the same day, the authorised officer—Martin Cosgrove—revealed that €50m had been invested in approximately 500 offshore insurance policies sold by National Irish Bank since 1991. By 8 June that figure had been revised to €63.4m and it led the Tánaiste to send Martin Cosgrove's report to the Director of Public Prosecutions.

There was at the time a momentum building in Ireland into the culture of corruption—Deposit Interest Retention Tax (DIRT) tribunals abounded and followed earlier judicial inquiries such as the beef tribunal. Now the new focus of attention was on the National Irish Bank.

Suddenly bank executives and staff were spending more and more time preparing the bank's defences from attack on two fronts.

The terms of reference of the High Court inspectors were widened to include the offshore insurance products whilst a group of National Irish managers and senior executives appealed to the Supreme Court a decision by the High Court that they must answer questions put to them by the National Irish Bank inspectors.

But the Supreme Court upheld the earlier High Court decision that staff and former staff had to answer questions put by the inspectors. The court also ruled that any confession obtained by the inspectors under the powers of the Companies Act would not be admissible in any subsequent criminal trial.

A firm of solicitors issued a statement on behalf of a number of National Irish Bank managers saying that they acted at all times in accordance with the directions of their employers. The managers said they welcomed the Supreme Court ruling, which left the way open for them to co-operate fully with the inspectors.

Clearly battle lines were being drawn—even within the National Irish Bank.

The bank's next court challenge was an attempt to stop the High Court inspectors from investigating its compliance with DIRT. The High Court rejected the bank's demand.

The court also rejected the bank's claim that it should be entitled to see copies of transcripts and documents arising from interviews conducted by the inspectors with bank staff.

It was clear the bank was being dragged kicking and screaming to co-operate with the High Court inspectors. In fact, in July 2003 —over five years after the inquiry began—the High Court was told that the inspectors' work was being delayed by a lack of co-operation from bank personnel against whom adverse findings were likely to be made. At the same time the bank was presented with an interim report from the inspectors.

Seven months later, in February 2004, the High Court expressed concern over the length of time the bank was taking to respond to the inspectors' interim report.

All the while the bank was attempting to present to the public the image of a caring bank. It set up its own inquiry into the overcharging. The report was completed in March 1999 by Colin Dundas—at the time regional manager, banking audit.

He checked out the integrity of the bank's systems to establish if unjustified fee or interest loading would have been controlled if bank procedures had been followed. He found:

> Full adherence to the bank's laid down procedures would have ensured that 'unjustified loading' of interest and fees could not have occurred. However, the systems catered for manual adjustments to be made to correct genuine errors and to apply interest resulting from the practice of 'suspending' customers' cheques to allow them time to introduce sufficient funds into their account to allow these cheques to be presented and paid.
>
> This process along with the relatively common practice of producing 'redo' statements, which appears to have been originally motivated by a desire to hide genuine mistakes from customers in order to present a more professional image, rendered the interest charging system vulnerable to

abuse. It is apparent from the work performed that some
degree of abuse was present and that the control mechanisms
in place were not always sufficient to either detect or prevent
this activity.

And if it wasn't bad enough that the bank's internal processes
were not up to the job of protecting customers from abuses,
Dundas then had to report that the practice had been picked up
by internal audits. These are his damning words: 'Both interest
and fee charging practices were part of the regular audit
programme applied for each branch visit and departures from
bank policy were regularly reported. Indeed, the substance of
some of the allegations being examined in this review emanated
from internal audit reports from the time.

Independence appears to have been maintained and findings
from audits performed were brought to the attention of
management up to Chief Executive level. However, the
'interest loading' findings in particular were not reported to
either the National Irish Bank board Audit Committee nor
[sic] Group Audit and this must be seen as a failing.

Hardly reassuring behaviour! The internal audits identifying
'abuses' had been brought to the attention of management right
up to the level of Chief Executive. But nothing was done. So, long
before the High Court inquiry could come to any conclusions,
the bank's own review process revealed failings in senior
management.

These failings might be considered trifling in the global
finances of the National Australia Bank. But what is more
significant is the rather casual attitude to the mismanagement of
interest and fee charges by a number of branch managers that
went uncorrected for some time by senior management. Money
is king. Even if it is somebody else's money.

Dundas also examined the management response to reports of
unjustified fee and interest loading. He determined that the only
significant internal audit reporting of unjustified loading related

to interest charges rather than fees. And while he recognised that management appeared to be bringing an end to these 'unsatisfactory practices', he noted: '. . . no attempts appear to have been made to make good any loss to the customers affected nor does any disciplinary action appear to have been taken against the managers concerned.'

While this report by Colin Dundas was being prepared, the bank had announced—on 4 August 1998—that it would pay IR£131,166 plus interest to 370 customers arising from improper interest and fee loading. At the time the bank said the figures indicated that the practice was not aimed at boosting profits.

Now in his report, Colin Dundas looked at the scale and detail of unjustified fee and interest loading in the named branches— that is, those featuring in the bank's audit reports and others mentioned in the media. He concluded that over the period reviewed it was 'not possible to justify completely the interest amendments made for specific and discrete periods in thirteen branches.'

He continued:

> In total, these amounted to IR£135,000 though it should be recognised that, because of a lack of full documentation due to the period of time that has elapsed beyond normal retention periods, some of this amount could have been justifiable at the time. The total amount refunded to customers after applying the appropriate indexation is IR£557,000. No 'unjustified loading' was found in the remainder of the network.

Turning to the issue of fees, Dundas found that there were three branches where 'insufficient justification could be found for the level of fees charged. Work has still to be completed in the third of these branches but it is anticipated from the work completed to date that approximately IR£200,000 of amendments will be refunded which will amount to nearly IR£1m after indexation.'

These excess charges were obviously proving to be a costly expense for National Irish Bank. But then, of course, for some time they had been making money out of their ability to take money from their customers.

Dundas reviewed the current practices to test if unjustified loading was a continuing problem. In terms of interest charges he said that while aspects of the system still remain vulnerable to abuse, there have been no instances of unjustified loading since the start of the investigation.

In terms of fees, he identified that the charging practices have become significantly more automated since the period covered by the allegations.

Dundas went on to state:

> In summary, there are clear cases where unjustifiable amendments have been made to both the interest and fees charged to customers' current accounts. However, these appear to represent the initiatives of individual managers rather than an institutionalised policy to defraud customers. Greater clarity on their motivation may emerge once the interview process has been completed.

> There was undoubtedly a strong requirement from senior management to meet demanding targets and it could be that this was a strong influence on the actions of some of the individuals involved. However, given the relatively small absolute amounts involved over an extended period it is unlikely that there was a concerted executive effort to enhance bank profitability through the application of 'unjustified loading'.

> The total number of branches affected is fourteen, with approximately IR£335,000 of unjustified amendments being found. After indexation, reimbursements amounting to nearly IR£1.5m will be made to customers of which IR£557,000 has already been paid.

But you might expect someone from the bank to try to say there was no concerted executive effort to fleece customers to enhance profits. What else could they say? What this report does do, is confirm that RTÉ reporters were correct to push ahead with their stories—in face of a bank using the judicial system to try to stymie them.

Although the damning High Court report concentrated on National Irish Bank's policy of encouraging and facilitating tax evasion, it also examined the interest and fee charging allegations.

In endorsing the bank's own findings, Mr Justice Blayney and Tom Grace disclosed how branches calculated interest and fee charges on troublesome accounts.

They decided not to name branch managers or staff whom they interviewed, although to help us understand the 'loading' of charges they published comments made by employees explaining how they calculated charges.

There was a system of charging for bank transactions—processing cheques had set charges, as did most transactions on a normal working account. It was the manual charges that gave rise to the 'loading' allegations.

This is where an account was not running smoothly and required the attention of bank staff to try to regulate and administer it. Senior management told branch managers that they should take careful note of the time spent on troublesome accounts and charge accordingly—that is, base their costs on an hourly rate.

The High Court report identified from their interviews with bank staff that there was no formal system.

However, in their report, Mr Justice Blayney and Tom Grace provided us with a sample of the comments they heard during interviews with bank managers and other more junior staff. It was clear that whatever system was supposed to be in place to regulate interest and fee charges was in many instances either considered too difficult to operate or was ignored because of established custom and practice.

Take this exchange for example:

INSPECTOR: Have I understood you correctly to say that interest adjustment was a widespread practice within the bank?
MANAGER: I would have felt it was.

INSPECTOR: There has been a suggestion that the practice existed in only the five branches that were named.
MANAGER: That is totally incorrect.

No doubt comments such as this helped the High Court inspectors disagree with the bank's own report into interest loading. This is what they concluded:

> The inspectors do not accept that the Bank, on the basis of the work done, was entitled, because of the scope limitations on that work, to reach the conclusion that the practice of interest loading was not widespread within the Bank. The Inspectors do not disagree with the other conclusions of the Report as far as they go, but do not accept that the work done excludes the possibility that there were other incidences of improper interest charges in the branches reviewed or elsewhere in the branch network.

When it came to fee charging, those interviewed by the High Court inspectors held the general view that there was no system of estimating the cost of management time to customers. Most agreed it was a question of 'guesstimate'.

A couple of the bank staff interviewed referred to the pressure to maintain income through fees. One said: '. . . the guideline was the previous fee and there would have been a certain amount of fees to be got in that quarter so it would really have to be the same fee as the last time plus a little bit more.'

Another commented: 'On the fee, it was target driven. There is no doubt in my mind on that . . .'

One interviewee told the inspectors that the bank had no system to calculate management time 'other than the fact that we were told to obtain 125 per cent cost covered . . .'

Not surprisingly, the conclusion was that there was no system of working out charges and the way in which these charges were applied was improper.

It was the expectation that bank staff would follow the lead of those engaged in this practice that was damaging and unacceptable to individuals like Dominic. This casual 'custom and practice' philosophy went against the grain where Dominic was concerned. Just because others were doing it to maintain the level of profits from interest and fees did not mean he would follow suit.

'I really had a problem,' Dominic told me, 'it just was not acceptable to place charges on people who did not deserve them. But others were doing it as a matter of fact. I was on my own and it did create some difficulties for me but I had to withstand it. I was not going to change my mind.'

But the worst criticism of the bank and its procedures came in the damning comments made in relation to the bogus non-resident accounts.

What had been alleged by the RTÉ broadcasts in January and March 1998 was, of course, the starting point for the High Court investigators. Basically, National Irish Bank had been accused of effecting policies of life assurance on behalf of its customers with a number of companies in the Clerical Medical International Group (CMI).

Further, it was alleged that these were companies not authorised under European Union legislation to carry on the business of life assurance in the Republic of Ireland.

RTÉ also disclosed that in addition to CMI, policies were also effected for bank customers with Scottish Provident International Life Assurance Ltd with an address in the Isle of Man and with another company with an address at Guernsey in the Channel Islands.

The most significant allegations made in the RTÉ transmissions were that:

- Bank representatives gathered information on customers holding non-resident accounts, accounts in false names and customers with funds undisclosed to the Revenue.
- The identified customers were invited to participate in an offshore life assurance linked investment scheme with CMI.
- Most of the monies invested were re-deposited with the bank; for the account holders this had the effect that the nature of their original deposits, which in many cases was at

the risk of discovery by the Revenue, was transformed.

- Senior managers in the bank were aware that the offshore investment scheme was being used to help customers evade tax.
- Some senior managers of National Irish Bank encouraged customers to evade tax.

If this was true, the National Irish Bank was operating outside the law. And guess what? The High Court inspectors found that yes, indeed, the National Irish Bank had acted improperly and outside the law.

The bank had taken steps to frustrate the investigation—even going to the courts in the Isle of Man to block the High Court inspectors from seeing the books. National Irish Bank had obtained a licence there to operate a branch in 1991. The courts in the Isle of Man refused the inspectors' petition.

But they had ample evidence when they concentrated their efforts back home in Ireland. By talking to branch managers they gathered invaluable gems that demonstrated the kind of culture within the bank.

Under pressure to get deposits, the managers accepted non-resident accounts on the flimsiest documentation, as these examples of comments made to the inspectors reveals:

> [Prior to the Money Laundering Act] If the customer came in and stated that he was from wherever he was from . . . we wouldn't have carried out checks to authenticate his address.

> INSPECTOR: When you were opening a non-resident account, what procedure did you adopt to satisfy yourself that the person was in fact a non-resident?
> MANAGER: That they completed the form and signed it. I would say, being honest, nothing more than that.

Another manager spoke of his delight to see anyone coming into his branch with over a hundred thousand pounds. He told the inspectors he would not be running around the streets to check if they were resident or otherwise . . . not unless he was a next-door neighbour or a regular depositor.

Customers related how they were assisted by their friendly branch bank manager to conceal their cash from the eyes of tax inspectors. They used addresses in England or Australia or wherever whilst living in the Republic in order to register as non-resident, as this interview reveals:

> INSPECTOR: So at that stage then [in January 1987] what discussion took place with the bank . . . vis-à-vis opening a non-resident account?
> CUSTOMER: Yeah, well I am going to say this out straight. The manager, he said, 'why don't you open an English account, a non-residential [sic] account?'
> INSPECTOR: What benefit would he have put forward in relation to that?
> CUSTOMER: Well, he says you don't have to reveal it to the tax people.
> INSPECTOR: And who was that manager?
> CUSTOMER: [Manager name] was his name.

Some bank staff fully embraced this illegal scam . . . allowing customers to hold accounts using the local branch as an accommodation address. How far was the bank prepared to go to secure deposits of cash? What pressure was on the bank managers at branch level to maintain deposits? Were they so desperate that they would allow someone to have a non-resident account whilst living in Ireland and to use a 'care-of branch address' to accommodate the deceit?

Well, frankly, the answer is yes—some branch managers actually took cash deposits from residents of the Republic but in order to deceive the tax inspectors then permitted some of these customers to use the bank as an address of convenience.

And yes, the pressure to at least maintain if not increase the cash deposited at their branches was so intense they were compelled to tolerate situations where the bank was failing to comply with legislation regarding tax collection. At least, that's what many of them told the High Court inspectors. They said they opened and maintained bogus non-resident accounts because:

- They wanted to gain or retain deposits as branches were under pressure to increase deposits and were struggling to do so. Competition from other banks meant that the only way to gain or keep a deposit was to agree it should be DIRT-free.
- They wanted to preserve a business relationship with a valuable customer who was threatening to withdraw his business unless facilitated.
- They knew that in the culture of the time, closing an account because it was bogus would not have been accepted as a good reason for losing the deposit.
- The inspectors provided examples of the bank managers' comments. They all seem to stress the fear of losing business:
- Under the pressure to increase the business I was happy to do it.
- . . . you didn't query them to an extent because you were under pressure to get deposits.
- I am aware that I did facilitate a couple of customers with non-resident status which, in hindsight, I was not totally comfortable with but it was to protect a deposit that I felt would have been lost to one of my competitors . . .
- . . . I think we were scared, I would say, of losing business.
- On the one hand they're telling me to get it sorted out, on the other hand they're telling me to get the resources up.

This final comment raises the question about the knowledge of these bogus accounts higher up the management chain and what, if anything, they did about them.

The High Court inspectors established some astonishing facts. First of all, they discovered that the bank's internal audit system picked up on these accounts and raised questions. Circulars were sent to senior management but yet nothing appears to have been done to resolve the issue.

One former head of internal audit, Paul Harte, was interviewed by the inspectors, who had by now established through evidence from the Head of Audit that the failure to address the issue of bogus non-resident deposit accounts resulted from management inaction. Mr Harte was asked why it took time to sort out the accounts. He told them: 'In my view it was because of management inaction . . . I think there was a reluctance on management's behalf to lose that sort of money from the network.' This was, he added, because that was a significant amount of money.

So rather than risk losing some of the bank's valuable deposit base, senior management turned a blind eye to the fact that the bank was stepping outside the law by allowing these bogus accounts to continue in existence.

Furthermore, they established that branches began identifying bogus non-resident accounts as potential investors in CMI policies. The business of selling the policies rested with the Financial Advice and Services Division (FASD). Part of the sales pitch was to guarantee confidentiality from the Revenue Commissioners and that no probate requirements would arise if a trust were created.

This deliberate targeting of cash deposits held in bogus non-resident accounts—and also in fictitious and incorrectly named accounts—helped the bank improve its income because, of course, the policies would need to be 'managed' and that meant annual fees for the administration.

From as early as 1991 internal audit reports noted examples of non-resident declarations that were at variance with other branch records. The High Court inspectors quote from these circulated documents for 1991, 1992, 1993, 1994 and 1995.

And the inspectors established that these internal audit circulars were sent to senior management right up to the Chief Executive level. In fact, the inspectors named nine senior management figures—including former Chief Executives Barry Seymour and Jim Lacey—in their criticism of the overcharging.

The inspectors also named nineteen National Irish Bank executives in relation to their knowledge of and responsibility for improper practices at the bank that included the tax evasion as well as the improper charging.

Bogus non-resident accounts. Tax evasion. Overcharging. Some would call that theft. All done with the knowledge of senior management members who failed to take steps to bring the bank back into proper control. Money is king.

This was the bank Jim Lacey ran for a decade until April 1998.

Born in 1950 at Newport, Co. Tipperary, Lacey became the hard-nosed businessman who led National Irish Bank from the front. After leaving school in 1967, he briefly worked for the Munster and Leinster Bank (now the Allied Irish Bank). He moved into accountancy with Coopers & Lybrand after gaining a commerce degree at University College Dublin through night classes.

In 1976 he joined ACC Bank as internal auditor and remained there until the early 1980s when he joined Forward Trust as finance director. This was the finance company owned by the Midland Bank, who also owned the Northern Bank at the time.

By 1985 Lacey had been elevated to the post of Chief Executive of the Northern Bank in the Republic. When National Australia Bank took over the Northern Bank in 1987 and changed the name of the bank operation in the Republic to National Irish Bank, they appointed Lacey Chief Executive.

Lacey was told National Australia was an aggressive, customer-orientated bank and his challenge was to build National Irish from its position as a small bank into a serious player. Lacey relished the challenge and began making the larger banks take note of his abilities to persuade customers to switch accounts.

Lacey used his imagination and hard work to promote National Irish. He utilised the media to push his bank and to strike fear into his competitors. His high public profile was not for self-promotion, it was a reflection of the kind of management favoured by the Australian owners of National Irish.

Their marketing strategy was to present the human face of banking, and Lacey favoured speaking directly to the media himself rather than through the public relations department.

He put this public persona to best use when he made public pronouncements on interest rate cuts. The bank's senior treasury and money market managers were instructed to inform Lacey's office of any changes in money market conditions that would allow a cut in interest rates. When such circumstances arose, a meeting was convened of the bank's interest-rate committee, made up of Lacey and senior managers from marketing and treasury.

The committee would consider the cost benefit of any proposed cut in hard financial implications. It would take no account of the intangible goodwill or the long and short-term marketing benefits. But Lacey did. Once the decision was made to cut the interest rate Lacey would go public with the announcement.

He was presenting himself as the Chief Executive of a small bank that was prepared to benefit its customers at the earliest opportunity, and, by getting to that point first, it left the larger, financially stronger banks looking lost. Consumers and politicians loved the way National Irish managed this aspect of their business, as it gave them weapons with which to attack the bigger banks.

But in spite of his high profile, Lacey attempted to protect his wife and family from the public gaze—fearful of any attempted kidnapping. He had good reason to be cautious as it turned out.

For on 2 November 1993, it happened.

A gang of at least eight men—led by notorious criminal Martin 'the General' Cahill—arrived at the Lacey family home at Blackrock, Co. Dublin, in the early hours. Armed with handguns and a rifle, they forced the couple into the house at 1.30 a.m. as they arrived home from a function at Clonmel in County Tipperary.

Inside the house, the couple's four children—aged four to sixteen—slept as did the couple's 21-year-old babysitter. Eventually, the gang roused the children and babysitter. They, along with Joan Lacey, were removed from the house and taken to another location.

At 5 a.m. an unmasked man was brought into the Lacey home and was introduced to Jim Lacey as the grandson of another kidnap victim. This man was apparently being forced to collect a ransom for the safe return of the Lacey family and their babysitter. It was later established that he was in fact a member of the kidnap gang.

At ten the following morning, Jim Lacey drove with the unidentified man to Merrion Road in Dublin where they transferred from Lacey's car to a parked green van and then continued to the Andrew's Lane branch of the National Irish Bank where the ransom cash of around IR£250,000 was procured and handed over.

Almost six hours later the six kidnap victims were released in north inner city Dublin.

The bank was compelled to conduct a major review of its security procedures. The ransom paid to the kidnappers from the branch at Andrew's Lane was only a portion of the cash stored there and it was paid out only after telephone calls between senior National Irish staff in Dublin and National Australia staff in London.

Jim Lacey appeared on television a few days after his family's ordeal with a gash clearly visible on his head. He told reporters he was angry that his family had been subjected to what was an extremely traumatic experience.

'It was a horrific experience for all of us,' he said, adding: 'The good thing is that they are all safe and well, but when you're as young as six to go through that type of experience, I just don't know what it will be like going into the future for some of them.'

He didn't know it at the time, but his own future was far from certain.

Just five months after his terrifying kidnap ordeal, the bank unceremoniously fired Lacey. He took the issue to the High Court and very quickly secured a financial settlement reported to be worth £600,000, or £1m sterling, depending which report you wanted to believe, and he remained as a non-executive director of National Irish Bank—a position he held for over three years.

But such was his acknowledged ability in banking that he soon found gainful employment in a number of other businesses.

However, when RTÉ ran their stories in 1998 the government acted. Jim Lacey's term of office as the Chief Executive of the National Irish Bank was about to come under the six-year scrutiny of two High Court appointed inspectors. And he did not escape criticism in their damning report.

In fact, Lacey is one of nine former National Irish Bank managers—including another former Chief Executive, Barry Seymour—to face the wrath of the Director of Corporate Enforcement, Paul Appleby. Appleby applied to the High Court in July 2005 to have all nine disqualified as company directors. At the time of writing, these matters are still unresolved.

The others named in the petition are: Frank Brennan and Michael Keane, former general managers, retail banking; Dermott Boner and Kevin Curran, former heads of retail banking; Tom McMenamin, former regional manager; Patrick Byrne, former head of finance; and Nigel D'Arcy, former head of the Financial Advice and Services Division.

Paul Appleby, in welcoming the High Court inspectors' report, said:

> The Inspectors' findings largely confirm the thrust of the allegations made against the bank and the company in 1998. Despite this, the report is deeply disturbing in revealing the extent to which illegality and bad practice were tolerated (and to some extent encouraged) within the organisation between 1988 and 1998.

One senior bank official said the overcharging of customers had to be viewed in the context of the kind of leadership of National Irish Bank. He said:

> In order to fully comprehend what happened, you have to understand that Jim Lacey was a bully with a very forceful personality. He ruled with fear and, in an attempt to gain market share, National Irish charges were usually better than the market, but he had to have some way of recouping any lost fees. Senior management would have been well aware of what was going on from internal audit and inspection but did nothing about it.

So that's one of the major explanations as to why National Irish Bank ended up in disgrace. Its former high-flying executives faced being 'struck off'. Still, this course of action is preferable to the criminal charges that were considered possible.

But not all National Australia Bank employees were so fortunate. Jail beckoned for four disgraced bankers in Australia following yet another scandal to rock the bank.

Just as the High Court inspectors in Ireland were putting the finishing touches to their report, an Australian whistle-blower was about to expose a foreign exchange swindle that would cost the bank hundreds of millions, lead to a boardroom bloodbath and result in an investigation by the Australian Securities and Investments Commission.

On 14 January 2004 National Australia Bank suspended four traders in its foreign currency options desk for trading losses estimated at the time to be Au$185m but which might rise to as much as Au$600m. Eventually the losses would be established at Au$360m.

Coming on top of the massive losses in the United States and the scandal in Ireland of operating the bank illegally and improperly at a cost of almost £50m sterling in repayments to customers and footing the bill for the High Court investigation —this was the last thing National Australia Bank wanted to discover.

In June 2005, Luke Duffy, the 35-year-old former head of National Australia Bank's foreign currency options desk, was jailed for twenty-nine months for his role in the bank's Au$360m trading scandal.

Duffy admitted three charges of dishonesty.

At Victoria County Court, Judge Geoff Chettle referred to Duffy's deceptions as sophisticated, calculated and involving enormous amounts. Along with three other traders, Duffy was accused of falsely inflating profits on the trading desk to avoid the scrutiny of the National Australia Bank's management to preserve their jobs and receive bonuses.

Having made a loss of Au$5m on a trade in September 2003, Duffy reported to his bosses a profit of Au$42m. This led to Duffy and his co-accused receiving bonuses.

The judge told Duffy: 'The mixture of personal ambition, arrogance and corporate culture made you forget the legal responsibilities you had to the National Australia Bank, its management and its shareholders.'

He went on: 'You and your team saw yourselves as invincible and justified your criminal conduct by asserting that your principal motivations were to make money for the bank. That's no excuse.'

Duffy repaid his Au$129,000 bonus to the bank and co-operated fully with investigators. Duffy's three co-accused have yet to be dealt with in court. One of them, David Bullen from Victoria, spoke out publicly before he was charged but after he had been suspended. He told an ABC programme that management at least two levels above him knew about the trades and let them through. 'My boss was aware,' he said; 'his boss was aware.' He added: 'Other areas of the bank were aware of this type of thing. It is not like you can hide limits and stuff like that from the rest of the bank.'

He asserted that the bank's risk management division had the power to tell traders to cut their exposure. But he said they never did so.

The bank's Chief Executive Frank Cicutto sits on the risk management committee. Perhaps Mr Cicutto's attention was taken up with the problems the bank was having in the United States.

Whatever the reason, he was soon under fire for his performance in relation to this latest scandal closer to home, and his term in office was in danger of bringing shame in the hall of fame at the bank's headquarters in Melbourne.

It's there that every Chief Executive is commemorated. The hallways in the executive suite at Bourke Street display photographs and sketches and underneath are plaques listing the bank's total assets and net profits during the reign of each Chief Executive.

There's pride in the fact that these previous Chief Executives built Australia's biggest bank through sheer aggression and a commitment to take on the world.

The numbers recorded on the plaques amount to a report card on the performance of the bank under each of the Chief Executives—driven to success since its beginnings in 1858 by buying other banks.

But Frank Cicutto's plaque looks like breaking that lineage of success. His watch as Chief Executive is pockmarked with problems at home and abroad. Critics accused him of a series of costly gaffes—the Au$4bn write down on HomeSide in America; a Au$600m blow-out on a software project and the Au$132m exposure to the collapse of a bus company—not to mention the cost of the illegal and improper trading of the bank in the Republic of Ireland. The foreign exchange trading losses only seemed to compound his problems.

With his Irish bank, National Irish, under High Court investigation in the Republic and with the pending formal investigation of this latest setback in his foreign exchange trading activities at home in Australia, Frank Cicutto had to go.

As the Australian Securities and Investments Commission got their investigation under way, Cicutto fell on his sword a month after the rogue trading scandal was revealed—taking the bank chairman Charles Allen with him.

New Chief Executive John Stewart came in with one thing on his mind—a clear-out of staff he blamed for the embarrassing foreign exchange scandal.

Naturally, he started with the four traders at the centre of the mess. These are the four mentioned earlier that eventually went on to face criminal charges. But Stewart also sacked their supervisor and three senior managers. He said others had been shifted and some had been disciplined, although there was no indication of how many and whom.

Stewart was no doubt spurred on by the findings in a damning report by accountants PricewaterhouseCoopers—established immediately after the rogue traders and their losses were exposed. This initial report said the traders had exploited loopholes and weaknesses in the bank's systems to hide trading losses.

All of them had apparently virtually doubled their salaries through the bonuses of up to Au$265,000 they received through their sham transactions that falsified profits.

The report also found that the bank had rejected out of hand warnings of suspect transactions from another bank and also from the Australian Prudential Regulatory Authority. It recorded the amazing fact that it was only when a junior employee acted as a whistle-blower that the scandal finally broke.

Stewart's actions did not quell the outrage from public and shareholders alike. Nor did it stop a series of formal investigations into the bank's performance—the bank's trading losses were investigated by the Australian Prudential Regulatory Authority; the Australian Securities and Investments Commission and the Australian Federal Police.

Stewart pledged changes: 'It is totally unacceptable that employees of the National breach policies and control limits. From now on there will be a zero tolerance police towards unauthorised limit breaches.'

Troublesome customers in Ireland who went over their limit got overcharged. Yet the National Australia Bank allowed four rogue traders who thought they could outsmart the system to go way over their limits—putting the bank at extreme risk and placing it in last place in the world's top ten rogue trading losses.

The bank appeared to have learned little—if anything at all—from others like Barings and the Allied Irish Bank, to name just two.

Australia's financial watchdog reported that the country's biggest bank put profit before probity. The Australian Prudential Regulation Authority (APRA) said the bank had 'failed at every level' to implement proper controls on risk management.

Condemning the bank's lax controls, the regulator said the board had paid lip service to the importance of internal controls but failed to act on its pledges. The APRA report went on: 'Despite often asserting that risk issues were of such importance that they should be dealt with by the full board, the board paid insufficient attention to risk issues.'

Instead, the bank suffered from a profits-first culture which led line managers to neglect internal controls and known risk management concerns. The report revealed that during interviews with corporate and institutional banking staff, a frequently heard expression was 'profit is king'.

That was supported by evidence at subsequent court hearings involving the four rogue traders at the centre of the scandal. Papers lodged at Melbourne Magistrates Court revealed that National Australia Bank's foreign exchange was required by management to deliver Au\$37m profit. But as the 30 September deadline for the end of the financial year approached, the desk was showing losses of Au\$5m. The problem was resolved by setting up fictitious trades delivering a Au\$42m profit.

Though this might be seen as an outstanding example, it is apparently fairly typical of what's known in banking circles as 'profit smoothing', which in this instance the National Australia rogues—and many others in capital markets—say goes on all the time.

Luke Duffy—the convicted and jailed head of the options desk —said: 'The bank wanted to be very big and very aggressive in the way it approached the market. Traders will generally do whatever they are able to do to achieve what they need to.'

Duffy's argument was that the 'smoothing' was not something traders did by choice but a response to management pressure for profits. 'It was coming from above,' he alleged, 'we didn't want to do it.'

And that was a point Duffy's boss, Gary Dillon, agreed with as he told the court: 'I don't believe there were any express indications one way or the other except on two occasions where we were asked to smooth the profit and loss after the sale of the banks that National Australia Bank owned in the US.'

Frank Cicutto's reign may have been tainted by scandal and losses but his severance package created controversy and uproar. It led to Australian opposition parties to call on the government to introduce restrictions on 'golden handshakes'.

They were angered by Cicutto's package, which was made up of:

- Au$3.27m termination settlement including a payment in lieu of six months notice
- Au$4.5m share options
- Au£3m in annual pay leave
- Au$1.3m bonus
- Au$2m superannuation

That is quite a package for a man who suffered so many embarrassing setbacks during his watch over the globally ambitious National Australia Bank.

Little wonder politicians were up in arms. And what must the poor shareholders have thought about rewarding a man who reigned over such ignominious shortcomings at home and abroad.

Faced with the costs of the expensive failure in America; the costly and embarrassing failure in Australia; the settlement for Chief Executive Frank Cicutto and the costs of running National Irish Bank improperly and illegally, it is hardly surprising that National Australia Bank's global ambitions had to be re-defined.

To add to the bank's discomfort, profits tumbled following the foreign exchange scandal. In the six months to 30 September 2004, profits were half what they were a year earlier at Au$1.2bn. The bank said there were no 'quick fixes' and that it would take until mid-2005 to recover.

Something had to be done and so the bank decided to slash 4,200 jobs over two years. At home in Australia 2,500 jobs would be cut, it announced early in 2005—that included about 400 staff in Asia where the bank will close its institutional markets and services offices in Singapore, Korea and Malaysia and shut its Tokyo securities company.

At the same time National Australia Bank announced plans to close 100 United Kingdom branches of the Clydesdale and Yorkshire Banks— cutting 1,700 jobs in the process.

In May 2005, National Australia posted a smaller than expected 12.5% fall in first half profits as it detailed plans to slash jobs.

Cash earnings before goodwill amortisation and one-off items for the six months up to 31 March 2005 fell to Au$1.618bn from Au$1.850bn a year earlier. First half net profits rose 17% - largely due to a Au$1bn profit from the sale of National Irish Bank and the Northern Bank.

National Australia Bank had good reason to be grateful to their Irish banking venture. The Northern Bank was the steady rock of profit in this sea of financial uncertainty.

The Northern Bank might have been small in stature, but it provided the Australians with a very good return on their capital investment in 1987.

Let's take a closer look at the Australians' seventeen-year tenure in Northern Ireland.

One senior management figure I spoke to said that of the £408m the Australians paid for the Clydesdale Bank, the Northern Bank and Northern Bank (Ireland)—only £150m was for the two strands of the Irish bank.

But he had an even more startling claim to make. He told me that when the purchase was going through, National Australia Bank began the due diligence process. This means the Australians were entitled to examine the bank's books—most particularly the loan book.

The man responsible for the due diligence process on the Clydesdale Bank's loan book was Don Argus, but it is not clear if he took part in the same operation on the Northern Bank's loan book.

The outcome was that staff at the Northern Bank were instructed to look at all the accounts to re-assess them and to raise provisions on them. Accounts at the Northern Bank were graded into three categories:

- Sub-standard—these were accounts that showed no profits for one year and where repayment might be a problem.
- Doubtful—no profits for a couple of years and with issues relating to the company that required to be watched closely. Dependent on security held for repayment.
- Loss—full repayment from profits and bank security unlikely and therefore requiring a provision to cover the shortfall.

As I understand it from one bank source, the Australians wanted the 'sub-standard' accounts to be pushed into the doubtful category and the 'doubtful' accounts to go into the 'loss' files.

In other words, thanks to this act of due diligence, the Australians had the bank increase the amount set aside to cover potential losses on risky accounts by £60m. This meant that in reality the Australians got the two strands of the Northern Bank for just £90m.

Selling the Northern and National Irish Banks for £967m meant that after seventeen years the Australians made a tidy profit on their capital investment amounting to a cool £877m.

Then there are the dividends taken over the seventeen years. These totalled £737.3m. The only year the Australians did not take a dividend was in 1993 when it acknowledged in the accounts that this was because of the 'special' dividend of £100m the previous year.

In total, the Australians removed in cash from the Northern Bank a total of £1,614.3m—or almost £1.62bn. That's certainly good business. The cash cow had produced enough milk to sate the appetite of the Australians—a fact acknowledged by National Australia Bank.

Announcing the sale, the National Australia Bank Chief Executive John Stewart told reporters: 'This is an excellent outcome for the National. We have achieved an attractive price for these banks, generating a significant profit and strengthening our capital base. It also opens an exciting new chapter for the two Irish banks and for Danske.'

But the Australians left behind a bank with just fifty-nine branches and a reduced 30 per cent share of the market it once dominated in Northern Ireland and a bank desperately in need of financial investment and a morale-boosting change in management to rejuvenate the workforce.

As one former Northern Bank manager put it: 'When the National Australia Bank bought the Northern Bank (Ireland) Ltd and made it the National Irish Bank, it was the fourth biggest in Ireland but now it is nowhere near that elevated status.' Indeed, the National Irish Bank has as little as a 3 per cent share of the market in the Republic.

Mind you, just the act of the Australians selling up and shipping out created an immediate response at the Northern Bank headquarters just a week before the robbery.

'When news broke of the sale of the bank from the Australians to the Danes,' explained one frustrated Northern Bank official, 'head office was shaken with cheering and applause because the Aussies were finally leaving.'

What had led them to this extreme position of dislike for their employers?

The Australians had flattered to deceive when they arrived in Belfast by allowing the Northern Bank to continue as it had before. Then it made sweeping changes . . . many of which displeased staff but apparently suited more senior management figures.

But the loss of corporate business aside, there were other changes that caused the Northern Bank staff and customers to wonder where it would all end. There was a slow erosion of jobs. The number of employees peaked at around 2,400 in the mid-1990s. But at the time of the sale of the bank, the numbers were down to just over 1,500 according to the accounts for 2004. However, these figures do not cover the number of people employed by National Australia Bank Europe—around 500—giving the Northern Bank a current staff allocation of around 2,000.

For while it was squeezing as much profit as it could out of the Northern Bank, National Australia Bank was making judgements about cash-saving projects.

As one former senior member of staff at the Northern recalled:

One effect of the changes in management was the fact that those with keys to the cash centre had been reduced in seniority and as part of the cost reductions there were fewer staff, and more junior staff had to take on greater responsibilities. When it comes to saving on security the relevant question is: will this financial saving help us provide a better system? It does not follow that a saving of £100,000 will increase risk.

It may or may not. No one will ever know for certain. It's the £26m question!

09 | THE HUNT GOES ON

B y midsummer last year the police hunting the Northern Bank robbers were back in the headlines.

A front-page lead story in the *Belfast Telegraph* on 20 June 2005 was headlined: 'We'll not stop till we catch robbers.' Underneath a smaller headline: 'Police pledge six months on from £26m heist.'

The paper had an interview with the senior officer who had taken over leadership of the PSNI team of forty-five detectives involved in the investigation. Det. Supt Phil Aiken told the paper there was to be no let-up in the pursuit of the robbers. In the six months since the robbery he said hundreds of interviews had been conducted and thousands of hours of CCTV footage from all over Northern Ireland had been screened, as well as painstaking forensic tests and banking checks. In all, the police had carried out 3,600 actions relating to the robbery.

He told the *Telegraph*'s crime correspondent, Jonathan McCambridge:

> Our investigation has brought to light a number of suspicious activity reports from banking institutions all over the world. We have investigated transactions to ascertain if any of the stolen money is being channelled through international bank

accounts. This is passed to our economic crime bureau who carry out the investigations. These inquiries have been conducted throughout the UK and Ireland as well as across Europe, in America and in Australia. Our investigations have shown that no money attributable to the Northern Bank robbery has yet been found. This shows that the national and international banking systems have been successful in identifying where Northern Bank notes are entering the system but we have checked them all out and they are not the stolen notes.

In what read like a mid-term school report aimed at boosting public confidence in the investigation which up to this point had not produced a single arrest, the police also pointed out that none of the £16m of new notes had turned up anywhere except the £50,000 at the sports club in Belfast used by police. Supt Aiken said the police believed that £3m of used sterling notes seized by Gardaí in Cork came from the bank robbery.

Warning that the police investigation would not be downsized as it still remained a priority for the PSNI, Supt Aiken said he was convinced the robbery was an IRA operation, adding:

We believe it was committed by terrorists with a high degree of professional knowledge who are proficient in avoiding detection by way of forensic and witness evidence. This is a massive logistical operation for us but it is being conducted in a professional way.

Given what was to follow a few months later, perhaps the most telling comment from Supt Aiken was this one:

We are looking at several different crime scenes in County Down and in Belfast. We are optimistic. This has been an extensive inquiry and we have deployed numerous resources as we endeavour to progress it.

But even as the police continued to hunt for the bank robbers and prepared to make their first arrests, the Northern Bank was plunged into even deeper despair . . . for its headquarters had been 'robbed' a second time.

This time the raiders used a sports bag and a trolley to remove the loot. It was a carbon copy of the pre-Christmas 2004 raid and it was taking place in the autumn of 2005. Most worrying for the bank was that, in spite of all the changes to security that had been implemented since the first raid, the second one went off without a hitch! The only difference between the two raids was that the second one was carried out by bank staff as a security test and no money was taken.

This is how one bank worker described it to me in October last year:

> The bank is presently carrying out a review of where it will locate its cash centre in light of the raid. The choice is to keep it at headquarters, or build a new centre, or move to an existing facility run by a security company at Mallusk on the outskirts of the city where other banks have recently shifted their cash centres. In the meantime, the new boss of the cash centre at headquarters decided to set up a security test. He himself loaded up a trolley—like the ones used in the robbery —with boxes and he disguised them by putting plastic bags on top. He got in touch with security and told them he was bringing up a trolley with rubbish. He buzzed the security doors internally and they let him through the sterile area. Then he pushed the trolley right up into the bullion bay. He told them he had to take it on to the street. They opened the doors. He left the building. Outside he removed some of the boxes from the trolley and placed them in his car. He made off. No one stopped him.
>
> Meanwhile, at around the same time, his deputy tried another manoeuvre. He packed a plastic bag of the kind used by Securicor to transport money with newspapers. He carried it through security and walked out the front door in the same way Ward had removed the £1m sports bag of cash. This happened only the other day and is top secret.

Such a security lapse is staggering and it seems likely to have a serious influence on the decision-making process. If anything, it is likely to encourage the bank to move its cash centre operation to more secure premises where the responsibility for security rests with the host security company.

It was not long after the bank's internal security test that the police were back in the headlines again. It was early November when a large force of uniformed officers arrived unannounced in the small, staunchly republican County Down village of Kilcoo, in the shadow of the Mountains of Mourne. The police moved in close to midnight on 1 November to search the home of 23-year-old building contractor Dominic McEvoy. With McEvoy under arrest and in custody for questioning, the police set about searching his home.

His parents told reporters that Dominic had arrived home from work around 11.20 p.m. and that the police arrived shortly afterwards armed with a warrant to search the semi-detached house in Mullandra Park in Kilcoo. Dominic McEvoy was arrested and taken away for questioning as the search began.

At the same time, the police also arrived at the door of 26-year-old Peter Morgan in Kilcoo. His home was searched and he too was arrested for questioning, although he was later released without charge. Peter Morgan's brother and Dominic McEvoy are business partners.

Two days later, on 4 November, Dominic McEvoy appeared in court—the first person to be charged in connection with the bank raid. He was accused of robbery, false imprisonment of a bank worker and his wife and having a gun or imitation firearm. McEvoy denies all the charges. In court a detective said the case was based on circumstantial and forensic evidence.

Det. Insp. Sean Wright informed the court that when charged on 3 November, McEvoy had replied: 'I had no involvement in the Northern Bank robbery or the kidnapping.' The police officer claimed that McEvoy's DNA was found on a hat at bank official Kevin McMullan's home in Loughinisland. As McEvoy was being removed from the courtroom, a large group of men in the public gallery started to applaud and shout encouragement.

McEvoy was remanded in custody to Maghaberry Prison in County Antrim.

The search and arrest operation at Kilcoo marked a sustained period of police activity over the next few weeks in relation to the bank raid. Other arrests quickly followed in Belfast and in County Tyrone. The second person charged was 42-year-old Martin McAliskey, from Ballybeg Road, Coalisland. He was charged with attempting to pervert the course of justice in relation to the purchase, possession and sale of a white van used in the robbery. The self-employed salesman denied the charges in court and was released on bail.

A 30-year-old British Telecom worker from Newry in County Down was the next to be charged. Computer technician Peter Kelly denied two charges of making and having documents likely to be of use to terrorists. The charges related to an unauthorised document on his work computer allegedly identifying 36,000 Northern Ireland civil servants, plus 3,300 who worked for the Police Service of Northern Ireland and 70 prison service employees. A Belfast court heard that when charged, Kelly replied: 'I refute and deny absolutely these hysterical and paranoid charges.' Described in court as a skilled computer technician who worked at Rosepark House in Belfast, Kelly was remanded in custody.

The day Kelly appeared in court, the Chief Constable, Sir Hugh Orde, was appearing at the House of Commons in London before the Northern Ireland Affairs Committee, along with his Deputy Chief Constable, Paul Leighton. The pair were quizzed about the Northern Bank robbery and, in particular, were questioned about the recent spate of arrests. Would there be more and did the Chief Constable believe that given the lack of intelligence about the robbery, could he prevent such incidents happening again?

Here's what Sir Hugh Orde said in response:

> In terms of the Northern Bank robbery, the first thing to remind everyone here, because it tends to get forgotten in the amount of money, is that this was a particularly brutal crime.

It could have been a murder. The abduction of people and the way they were treated was utterly brutal. This was not some Robin Hood effort, this was a really brutal crime.

In terms of the police arrests, yes, it shows we were determined to solve it, and the most effective way of solving it is to bring people in front of the courts. Three people currently stand charged with offences relating to the Northern Bank. As a result of the arrests we have made, a number of other people, I am confident, will be arrested and hopefully charged in the future. Of course, not only are we looking at our main suspect—this was a very large operation run by the Provisional IRA involving a large number of people—but we are also looking at any other opportunity to arrest the suspects, if we can, for other offences where it is appropriate.

I am a great believer that if you cannot arrest someone for A, if you have got the evidence you arrest them for B and you take them out of circulation. It works. It works if you follow the money and it works if you follow other offences, and it works in Northern Ireland as well as it works in London. So hopefully we will see some more.

In terms of the intelligence issue, as I said, I was involved in the Stevens investigation and we were determined to make sure the intelligence structure in Northern Ireland not only was fit for the purpose but was well-organised and could stand any external test in terms of how we handle intelligence. There is a long history in Northern Ireland which has been used by many people just to discredit what is perfectly lawful, and it is always around intelligence-handling. We have a system now which I would defy anyone else in the United Kingdom to beat. In terms of our authority levels, for example, for participating informants, all those difficult issues which we have to deal with, we are seen as best practice. That is not me, that is the Surveillance Commissioner saying that. He commended our structure to make sure that we complied fully with the Regulations Investigatory Powers Act when dealing with these difficult issues in terms of registration and participation. So I am happy that this was not an intelligence failure.

Any crime *per se* is an intelligence failure, be it here, be it in London, or be it anywhere else. If we knew about it, we could stop it. I would say that the intelligence picture in Northern Ireland is sometimes very complicated. Certainly at the time this bank robbery was going on, all sorts of other things were going on. So what you see in hindsight makes a lot more sense than it does at the time. But it would be fair to say that these arrests are the result of substantial intelligence-gathering by my organisation.

Asked if he was saying that he could now see from intelligence he had, that there were things which with hindsight would have pointed him down a road which might have taken him some way towards preventing this kind of crime happening, Sir Hugh said:

No, I am not saying that. What I am saying is that some things make more sense. Whether you would ever stop something that was planned by an organisation which has got thirty years' experience of doing this sort of thing—on the notion that this was the first bank robbery committed by the IRA, let us remind ourselves that the IRA have committed bank robberies as well as murders and bombings for the last thirty-five years. This was not a sudden change.

Deputy Chief Constable Paul Leighton told the committee:

I was involved in intelligence-gathering in the RUC in the past and I would honestly say our intelligence capability now is much superior, not just in gathering it but in what we do with it when we have got it. That is not to say it was bad in the past, but everything develops and everything moves on.

The Chief Constable was right. There were more arrests. In all, twelve people were brought in for questioning—of which three had been charged by this stage. Among those arrested, questioned and released without charge was forty-year-old leading republican, Brian Arthurs from Dungannon in County Tyrone.

He, like many of the others who found themselves in a similar position, condemned the police actions as heavy-handed. The police were also accused of making political arrests.

But then came the biggest surprise of all, almost three weeks after the Chief Constable's appearance at the House of Commons, with the arrest of Chris Ward—one of the Northern Bank staff held hostage by the robbers almost a year before.

This was the 23-year-old bank supervisor who had gone public to speak about his ordeal on BBC television and in an interview with the *Irish News*. Now here he was, being quizzed by detectives about the robbery.

A squad of police officers arrived at Ward's home in Poleglass —where gunmen had held his family hostage during the robbery. After arresting Ward they began a detailed search, removing a number of items belonging to the bank supervisor. At the same time his girlfriend, Seanin McKenna, was arrested for questioning as well, although she was later released without charge.

When Ward appeared at Belfast Magistrates' Court in December last year, it was after eight days of questioning during which time there were fifty interviews with the bank employee who had only returned to work a few weeks before his arrest.

The court heard that the case against Ward was based on four main areas—his actions on 18 and 19 December; his actions on 20 December, the day of the robbery; his original account of what happened and a works rota.

Det. Insp. Sean Wright said in court that he could connect the accused with the robbery and he added that surveillance would have a direct impact on at least one of the four areas he had outlined.

Ward made a lengthy statement of denial when he was charged and it was read out in court. In it he said:

> Police have bugged my house, a holiday in Spain, went through all my phone records, my bank accounts, hounded my friends, even going as far as Australia and have tortured my family in an attempt to frame me with the Northern Bank robbery. Police have failed in all of these counts. They have

held me longer than the hostage-takers who seized me last year, and indeed have held me in a police station for longer than anyone else in the history of the North of Ireland.

This last point was a reference to a 48-hour extension granted to police to continue questioning Ward after he had been in custody for a week. The police application succeeded in court—making Ward the first suspect to be held for more than seven days since the introduction of the Terrorism Act 2000. The decision to grant the extension was challenged immediately by Ward's legal team, on the grounds that Ward and his solicitor were excluded from part of the hearing before a Crown Court judge on 6 December 2005. They were asked to leave while a senior detective detailed five areas of questioning they wished to put to Ward if granted the 48-hour extension.

Next day, Frank O'Donoghue QC, representing Ward, told the High Court that Ward should be released because the judge at the lower court had exceeded the remit of the Terrorism Act 2000. He argued that this was the first time that a suspect in Northern Ireland had been held for more than seven days and there was a need for the judicial authorities to do things correctly. He added: 'I regret to say that the judge manifestly failed to do so.' Mr Justice Hart turned down the application stating that the judge in the lower court had acted properly.

Ward remained in custody until 21 December when he returned to the High Court and was granted bail—exactly a year and a day after the robbery. He was released on bail, which was set at £10,000, with two sureties of £10,000 and £45,000 each from Ward's parents with the title deeds to their home as security—putting the total for bail at £120,000. Lord Justice Campbell ordered him to report to police twice daily, observe a curfew and surrender his passport. Ward was also ordered not to go within a mile of the scene of the raid.

The prosecution objected to bail during the one-hour hearing when Ward appeared via a video link. Gordon Kerr QC, for the prosecution, claimed witnesses or evidence could be interfered with and Ward might not turn up for his trial. Mr Kerr also referred to Ward's attitude while in the home of fellow bank employee Kevin McMullan in Loughinisland, stating that it could be described as 'strange'. He went on: 'He made a request to the hostage takers to get him some beer from the fridge and slept through part of the evening.' Mr Kerr then told the court that when left alone with Mr McMullan next morning, Ward strongly and vehemently resisted Mr McMullan's suggestion that they use the helpline supplied to bank workers.

Mr Kerr went on:

> Despite the fact McMullan was the senior person, he had no further contact with the robbers and all contact went through Ward, whose behaviour again appears to be inconsistent that threats were made. After the first pick-up of cash it was observed that the driver spoke in whispers to Ward and handed him wrapping materials to put around cages of money to be loaded. The evidence suggests the knowledge shown by the robbers of the internal systems in the bank made it clear they had inside knowledge and that was consistent with Ward's duties, not someone higher in the bank.

But for Ward, Mr O'Donoghue said: 'His clear case is that he has been a victim of this group and was not a participant in any way, shape or form.'

Lord Justice Campbell said Ward had to be presumed innocent until proven guilty. He said: 'This case is one of circumstantial evidence and it is not my task to comment on the strength or weakness of that.' He went on to say Ward had a clear record—as did his parents with whom he lives. The judge did not accept the prosecution argument that Ward would not turn up for his trial. In granting bail the judge said he was influenced by the fact Ward had a clear record and was considered fit for a place of responsibility with the bank.

Police on both sides of the border continue their investigations. As we go to print, the Garda file into the alleged laundering of the proceeds of the Northern Bank raid is due to be handed over to the Director of Public Prosecutions.

Meanwhile, the £26m Northern Bank raid has lost its unwelcome position as the biggest cash robbery in British history with the £53m robbery of a Securitas depot in Tonbridge in Kent early in 2006.

What's interesting about the English robbery is that there was an immediate posting of a £2m reward. There was no such offer in the Northern Bank case. It would be pure speculation to link the rapid progress of the English police investigation to the 'reward factor' but they certainly moved quickly to charge five people and bring them before the courts there. It would also be pure speculation to wonder if the posting of a reward in Northern Ireland might have assisted in a better result in the Northern Bank investigation.

APPENDIX

Making Northern Ireland Safer For Everyone Through Professional, Progressive Policing

Police are investigating the robbery that occurred at the Northern Bank, Monday 20th December 2004. Even If you are unable to help, it would be greatly appreciated if you could complete this form and return it through your supervisor / manager.
In relation to this investigation can you assist with any of the following?

1. In December 2004 were you based at the Northern Bank Donegall Square West Belfast?

2. If so Please complete the following: -

   Your Name _____

   Your work Location _____

3. Were you working in Northern Bank Headquarters Donegall Square West Belfast on 20th December 2004?

   Hours you worked _____

   Or reason for absence _____

4. Were you outside the bank building for any period of time between the hours of 6.00pm and 8.15pm? Or did you leave the Bank to go home between 6.00pm and 8.15pm?

   If yes answer questions below
   If no go to Question 14

5. Were you in the area of Wellington Street / Upper Queen Street / Howard Street / Wellington Place / Queen Street between 6.00 pm and 7.00 pm on Monday 20th December 2004?

6. If so, did you see a male carrying an Umbro sports bag which was black with a green flash?

7. Did you see a male in Upper Queen Street wearing a scarf and having a hat pulled down over his face between 6.00 pm and 7.00 pm on the 20th December 2004?

8. Between 6.00 pm and 7.00 pm on Monday 20th December 2004 did you see two men sitting in a bus shelter in Upper Queen Street? One of these men then walked off with the Umbro sports bag.

9. Do you recall seeing a female described as
Late 50's approx 5' 6" - 7", heavy build short dark hair unkempt with slight natural wave and left parting. Round faced with hard mannish features ruddy complexion square jawed. Staring dull eyes, thin lips. Mannish hands. Wearing dark shoes trousers and 3/4-length coat.

Around the Bus Stop outside the Northern Bank Building Donegall Square West, talking on a mobile phone and staring down Wellington Street between 1930 and 1940 hours?"

10. Were you in the area of Wellington Street / Upper Queen Street between 7.00 pm and 7.15 pm on Monday 20th December 2004?

11. If so, did you see a van reversing from Upper Queen Street into Wellington Street?

12. Were you in the area of Wellington Street / Upper Queen Street between 8.00 pm and 8.15 pm on Monday 20th December 2004?

13. If so, did you see a white van drive from Wellington Street into Upper Queen Street?

14. Have you any information regarding events surrounding the Robbery that you can forward to the Police.

If you have any queries please contact the Incident Room at North Queen Street.

Telephone 02890 650222, ext 16201, 16397, 33804

Direct Line 02890 561804

Crimestoppers 0800 555 111

Thank You